T0159501

Richie Ashburn ....
Why the Hall Not?

The Amazing Journey to Cooperstown

BY
BRUCE E. MOWDAY
AND
JIM DONAHUE

BARRICADE
BOOKS

Published by Barricade Books Inc.
185 Bridge Plaza North
Suite 309
Fort Lee, N.J. 07024
www.barricadebooks.com

Library of Congress Cataloging-in-Publication Data

Richie Ashburn—why the Hall not? : the amazing journey to
Cooperstown / by Bruce E. Mowday and Jim Donahue.
    p. cm.
  Includes bibliographical references and index.
  ISBN-13: 978-1-56980-450-6 (hardcover : alk. paper)
  ISBN-10: 1-56980-450-8 (hardcover : alk. paper)
1. Ashburn, Richie 2. Baseball players—United States—Biography.
3. Baseball announcers—United States—Biography. I. Donahue,
Jim. II. Title
  GV865.A79M69 2011
  796.357092--dc22
  [B]
                                                          2011013834
                    ISBN 13: 978-1-56980-450-6
                         1-56980-450-8

                     10 9 8 7 6 5 4 3
          Manufactured in the United States of America

Richie Ashburn . . . . Why the Hall Not?: The Amazing Journey to Cooperstown is dedicated to everyone who enjoys America's national sport and to the players who make the games so enjoyable. The book is also dedicated to those players who take the time to sign an autograph and say a few kind words to young fans. Richie Ashburn was a model of what a fan's player should be and Richie should be emulated by the stars of today.

TABLE OF CONTENTS

FOREWORD

IN THE COURSE of a person's life there are many influences . . . people who make an impact on how we think, how we act, how we go about our lives. Many times those who influence us are close to us. They can be parents, siblings and teachers. Perhaps it is someone in the community who helps make a difference in the world we reside.

Then there is a certain group of persons we don't know personally but we admire for their words and deeds. Quite often they are celebrities, actors, musicians, writers, politicians, and athletes. Rarely do we get to meet these celebrities, let alone really know them. Yet we tend to generously label them with the title of hero. This is especially true in our youth.

The following story is a tale of a young boy who got to meet his hero. It was a brief encounter, but it left a lasting impression. Years later, that small spark of time led to a relationship that benefited both men . . . in ways that neither could have imagined when they first met.

The "hero" in this book was a hero to many people, especially in the Philadelphia metropolitan area. His name was Richie Ashburn, All-Star centerfielder for the Philadelphia Phillies. He had movie star looks to go along with his incredible athletic ability. For the decade of the 1950's, he was one of the premier players in the game.

When his playing career was over he nearly returned to his home in Nebraska to pursue a life in politics. He chose instead to try his hand at broadcasting. Nebraska's loss was Philadelphia's gain. For almost 35 years he entered the homes of Phillies' fans on a nightly basis, illustrating the game and entertaining with his dry Midwestern wit and humor.

My first encounter with Richie came in 1982. I had been hired by the Phillies as a video coordinator for the ball club that winter. As a lifelong Phillies' fan, this was a dream come true . . . to report to Clearwater, Florida, for the first day of spring training. I had met broadcaster Chris Wheeler earlier that winter, and he told me to meet him for dinner that night at the famous Beachcomber restaurant.

I began a strange, new, and sometime intimidating job. My first night I was sitting next to Richie Ashburn at a large table filled with his old friends. Richie immediately made me feel comfortable, one of the "family." He used the term often and accurately to describe the Phillies' organization. It was a memorable night, one that would set the tone for my next 28 years with the ball club.

During the years that followed, Richie Ashburn was always a constant. He was approachable, funny, and never seemed self-important. If there was an empty seat in the cafeteria, Richie would use it regardless of those who occupied the rest of the table. They could be executives, ground crew or janitors. He would break bread with all of them. He often entertained his tablemates with a story or anecdote. To the Phillies' staff, he was simply a co-worker . . . not "The Great Richie Ashburn." He never carried himself that way, and did not expect to be treated as such.

Upon his death in 1997, I began to collect interviews about Richie with the hope of someday producing a documentary about his life. His colleagues, friends, family members, and old teammates passing through Philadelphia were included in this project. They each gave a small glimpse of this great man. The real impetus for the documentary came when his son Rich Ashburn, approached me with a box of old film that contained home movies of his playing days and hometown of Tilden, Nebraska. After a trip to Tilden in the summer of 2007, it was time to make this production happen.

In the course of writing and shooting for *Richie Ashburn – A Baseball Life*, I remembered a story about a man who started a grass roots campaign to get Richie elected to the Baseball Hall of Fame in Cooperstown, New York. At first it was difficult to find him. Fortunately, he found me.

Jim Donahue had heard about the project and asked to be a part of the documentary. He gave a great interview. He told a wonderful story. As a young boy, a chance encounter with Richie led Jim to a lifetime admiration of the Philadelphia icon. As an adult, he had something to give back.

As Ashburn's baseball career came under careful review, it became apparent that his statistics were good enough to warrant consideration for the Hall of Fame. A change in the rules of eligibility, however, had removed Ashburn from consideration. It was not Richie Ashburn's nature to combat such an injustice, someone else would have to right the wrong. Jim Donahue was just the man to try.

On a baseball scale, Jim Donahue is much closer to a Tug McGraw than to a Richie Ashburn. Jim has that Irish, cockeyed optimist persona that is well suited for taking on windmills and achieving the impossible dream. His quest was fueled by the emotions created by his hero, a man who not only belonged in the exclusive club of the Hall of Fame because of his on field exploits but also because of his body of work that followed as an announcer during three decades of Philadelphia summers.

This book details the machinations of Jim Donahue's quest . . . to see Richie Ashburn inducted into the Hall of Fame. It is common knowledge that it came to fruition and Richie is included in the Hall at Cooperstown. What is most meaningful to me was that Richie was able to live to see it. Ravaged by diabetes, no one was aware of how poor Richie's health had become by the mid-90's. He only lived a few years past his induction.

It was clear to me after countless interviews with family and friends how much Cooperstown meant to Richie Ashburn. While he often downplayed his selection, even questioning his admittance in his own induction speech, it was clearly the greatest day and the greatest honor of his life. And the beauty of it was that Richie got to share it with the man who helped make it happen.

The following is a story of inspiration, dedication, determination, friendship and reward. And a happy ending that can't be beat.

Dan Stephenson
December 2010

A FAN'S MESSAGE

At the start, there wasn't anything about the summer of 1957 that would indicate the impact it would have on my later life. America still liked Ike. We were just over a decade removed from World War II. Dads worked, and Moms stayed home with the kids and the kids played ball. In my Southwest Philadelphia neighborhood, if you had a pimple ball and a broomstick, you had all the ingredients for a ball game. Stickball, hoseball, stepball, boxball it didn't matter, it was all baseball, and baseball was king.

The Phillies at that time were a perennial second division team which meant of the eight National League teams, they were usually in the bottom four. The promising team that was The Whiz Kids just seven years earlier was gone. There were of course the two shining stars in the otherwise black hole that was the Fightin' Phils. Ace right-handed pitcher Robin Roberts, and the speedy, hitting machine in centerfield, Richie Ashburn.

I was eight years old, and I was an Ashburn guy. As a present for my eighth birthday, my Dad got tickets for my first Phillies game, July 20, 1957, against the Reds. I remember the excitement, walking through the turnstile at Connie Mack Stadium. What really stands out were the smells. The smell of the real grass field, the hot dogs and the cigars. To this day, when I smell a cigar, I think of Connie Mack Stadium. The other thing that was spectacular? The Phillies were in color. Remember, it was '57, and I only knew the Phils by way of a black and white Philco television. Before the game that day, with an autograph book in hand, that I had bought at Woolworth's the day before, I got my first autograph, and it was from Richie Ashburn. Richie signed my book, and gave me a pat on the head. I don't think I said anything other than thank you. The experience probably lasted all of a minute or so, but to a young fan, it turned into a life-changing event.

The summer of 1991 I met Richie Ashburn again. He was still the same friendly, approachable guy I'd met as an eight year old. It seemed that a recent rule change had removed Richie from ever being considered for election to the Hall of Fame. Most baseball fans, myself included, believed the rule change was unfair. I truly believed one fan, rallying all of Richie's fans, could make a difference. That day the "Richie Ashburn . . . Why the Hall Not?" campaign was born.

The next four years would find me set up at Veterans Stadium to talk to fans, mailing thousands of letters and talking to any group or person that would listen. Over the course of those four years, people with much more knowledge, both marketing and baseball-wise, questioned my resolve and my sanity. Whitey himself said on more than one occasion he thought I was flogging a dead horse. I took all of that with a grain of salt, because there was something I knew that was undeniable. Richie Ashburn belonged in Cooperstown.

After gathering more than 180,000 signatures on petitions, and sending out thousands of "Why the Hall Not?" bumper stickers, on March 7, 1995, the word came down from Cooperstown. Richie was a Hall of Famer. One thing that I always wanted to stress was this: Richie Ashburn was always a Hall of Famer. My campaign was formed to overturn an unfair rule that kept him from consideration. The most valuable thing I received from those four years was a friendship with my boyhood hero.

In the years that followed Richie Ashburn's Hall of Fame induction, people would ask me to describe my feelings for

Rich. I think I can sum it up in two sentences. One of the greatest thrills of my life was to call Rich Ashburn my friend. One of the greatest honors of my life was to have him call me his friend.

By Jim Donahue
March 2011

The Autograph

THE SMELL OF fresh grass, a novelty for a city boy in the 1950's, was the first thing young Jim Donahue noticed as he eagerly strode into Connie Mack Stadium, the grand old ballpark at 21st Street and Lehigh Avenue in Philadelphia. Stale cigar smoke was the second.

Visits to Connie Mack, where the Phillies played for more than three decades, were special treats to Jim as a youngster. This was the era before every game was televised. The Sunday game was usually the only one that was broadcast. Jim's father obtained tickets three or four times a year, and Jim would anticipate each visit for weeks, excitement mounting as the big day approached.

"I remember the enormity of the park; at least it was to the eyes of a young fan," recalls Jim. "The stadium was expansive. You could see the park as you drove up Lehigh Avenue through the residential neighborhood. The architecture was great. The park looked a lot like the old Lit Brothers Department Store at Eighth and Market streets in Philadelphia. I saw a lot of sandlot baseball fields with lumps and bumps as a kid. Connie Mack Stadium was a park with a perfectly manicured field. I remember the cut grass and freshly lined field."

The Phillies was Jim's baseball team, even though The Whiz Kids' National League championship team of 1950 was fast fading into history when he began avidly following the team. He was only one year old when the Phillies met the New York

Yankees in the Fall Classic and Whitey Ford and the Yankees completed a sweep of the Phillies on October 7, 1950.

Some members of The Whiz Kids, including Robin Roberts and Richie "Whitey" Ashburn, were still on the roster when Jim started going to Connie Mack with his father and brothers. The durable Roberts seemed to pitch almost endless innings each season as he battled and baffled batters with his fastball and assortment of pitches. Jim's idol, Ashburn, as always, patrolled center field with speed and grace. On offense, Richie stole bases and drove opposing pitchers mad with his bat control. He had the ability to slash singles here and there and foul off pitch after pitch until he drew a walk or slapped a pitch past an opposing infielder. Richie was well on his way to becoming a legend in the City of Brotherly Love when Jim, from his perch in the left-field bleachers, watched him perform his baseball magic.

Jim remembers his father giving him tips on the proper way to play baseball by pointing out how the major leaguers went about their business. Jim was told to watch Richie as he positioned himself in the spot most advantageous to his catching a ball hit by an opposing batter.

And Donahue used those tips during his many neighborhood games. "I loved baseball; baseball was my sport as a kid. I played all of the time. I played all of the many versions of city ball, including half ball, pimple ball and box ball. I played ball all summer long. I stayed out until the sun went down almost every day. I played organized Little League, but mainly I played with my friends in the neighborhood."

* * *

When Connie Mack Stadium opened on April 12, 1909, it was known as Shibe Park, named for Benjamin Shibe, a partner, along with Connie Mack, of the historic Philadelphia Athletics ball club. In 1953 the park was renamed in honor of Mack. The park was the nation's first steel-and-concrete stadium and was designed and built in one year by William Steele & Sons, a prestigious Philadelphia company. When it was built, it was not only the nation's most luxurious ballpark but also the most expensive: it cost almost $500,000 to build. Even so, some unlucky fans in obstructed seats had to peer around steel posts to see the playing field.

The American League's Philadelphia Athletics first played in the park. The Phillies joined the A's in playing there in 1938. The A's moved to Kansas City in 1954 and the National League team continued playing at Connie Mack until Veterans Stadium opened after the 1970 season. After the final pitch was thrown, the grand old park, the setting for vivid memories of thousands of fans of Donahue's generation, sat vacant in the middle of a deteriorating neighborhood for six years. On August 20, 1971, a fire destroyed part of the structure. In June 1976, it was razed, and the site is home to the Deliverance Evangelistic Church.

"Connie Mack's old office was located over the entrance to the park. It was where he ruled the roost while he was with the Philadelphia A's," Jim said.

Mack, known as the grand old man of baseball, is a baseball legend who was elected to the Baseball Hall of Fame in 1937. He was the longest-serving manager in Major League Baseball and holds the records for wins (3,731) as well as losses (3,948) and total games managed (7,755). He managed the Philadelphia Athletics for 50 years before retiring at age 87 following the 1950 season. He was the first manager to win the World Series three times and is still the only manager to win consecutive World Series on two separate occasions (1910 and 1911, and 1929 and 1930).

Mack, who was born in 1862 and died in 1956, was also a National League catcher, playing for ten years before retiring in 1896.

* * *

Saturday, July 20, 1957, had all of the earmarks of being a special day in the young life of James F. Donahue. His father, James P. Donahue, had secured seats for Jim and his two younger brothers, Chris and Howard, to watch the Phillies take on the Cincinnati Reds. The trip to Connie Mack Stadium was part of a birthday celebration for young Jim. He had celebrated his eighth birthday the week before the game and the tickets were a birthday gift. Visits to see the Phillies were rare as the elder Jim Donahue worked for a trucking company, and the only time the family could visit Connie Mack Stadium was when he had a day off work.

"The year 1957 was the time I became a true baseball fan. I was eight years old. The Phillies were undergoing a lot of changes. The excitement of the championship season had faded and the Phillies were a mediocre ball club. They finished the season with a .500 record. The Phillies had their first African American player in John Kennedy, a decade after Jackie Robinson had broken the color barrier. Kennedy was a shortstop and made his debut on April 22, 1957. The Phillies also had rookies that finished one and two in the balloting for Rookie of the Year honors in pitcher Jack Sanford and first baseman Ed Bouchee," Jim said. "It was also the year Whitey hit the same spectator twice in the same at bat. It took place on August 17. The woman was taken to a hospital."

The inner-city stadium was in a rough neighborhood. Jim recalled, "I remember drivers paying insurance to some of the neighborhood youths waiting outside the ball park. It was the best 25 cents many fans ever spent. They would watch your car and make sure it kept all of the wheels and wasn't vandalized at the end of the game."

On the hot Saturday afternoon of July 20, 1957, the Phillies were hosting the Reds in the second of a four-game series. The Phillies had lost the Friday night game, 7-2, and would go on to lose both ends of a doubleheader on Sunday, 4-2 and 6-4. The starting pitchers for the Saturday contest were right-handers Hal Jeffcoat for the Reds and Jim Hearn for the Phillies. Jeffcoat began his Major League career as an out-fielder, but because of a low batting average and a strong arm he became a pitcher. Neither of the starting pitchers would last very long in the mid-day heat: Jeffcoat's day was finished after two and a third innings, while Hearn was gone after three and a third innings.

Jim's favorite player, Richie Ashburn, had a double in three at bats and scored a run. Pitcher Turk Farrell kept the Phillies in the contest by entering the game in the seventh and throwing three scoreless innings. The Phillies began the bottom of the ninth inning trailing 5-4. With one out in the ninth, Phillies manager Mayo Smith called on his ailing catcher, Stan Lopata, to pinch hit. Lopata, who had battled injuries the whole year, walloped a walk-off, three-run home run to win the game for the Phillies. The Reds' losing pitcher Don Gross had pitched six shutout innings before giving up the blow by Lopata. Gross's record fell to 4-6 for the season; Farrell's improved to 4-2.

The Reds and the Phillies finished in the middle of the standings in 1957. The Milwaukee Braves won the National League pennant that year while the Reds finished in fourth place, three games ahead of the fifth-place Phillies.

* * *

The victory was exciting but what Jim recalls mostly vividly about that July day at the ballpark happened minutes before the Phillies took the field. "Dad had a friend from church, Ross Miller. He worked in accounting for the Phillies. He told Dad to be at the park early and come down to the field near the Phillies' dugout. He said there would be an opportunity to gather some autographs.

"I remember going to Woolworth's to purchase an autograph book. It cost less than a dollar. I came to the game equipped with pencils. I should have been smart enough to have some pens. If the pencil points had broken, I would have been out of luck. The autographs in my books are in pencil.

"We went down to the field to the area of the Phillies' dugout. Richie Ashburn came over and signed my autograph book. It was such an exciting moment of my life. I'm not sure if it took longer than 45 seconds but it was a big deal to me. Richie, my sports hero, even said a few words; I can't remember exactly what he said but it was along the lines of, 'Enjoy the game.' He was such a nice guy."

Jim's father took a photograph of his son and Ashburn. The photo survived and later was used by the Phillies in a video about Ashburn's life.

"Richie was my favorite player, absolutely, without a doubt. At that time Richie and Robin Roberts were the players that offered fans hope for a victory. When Richie came over that day it was a great situation for me. There wasn't a crowd. Today, young fans usually have to fight through a throng to get an autograph when players are inclined to sign them. Today players are shielded from the fans. In the 1950's, the players lived in the neighborhood and even took public transportation to the games. They were more accessible and part of the community. I just remember Richie being so nice to me and my family. You don't see that from many players today."

* * *

Richie Ashburn would remain Jim's favorite player, even when Richie was traded to the Chicago Cubs and finished his career as a member of the expansion New York Mets. "I have to admit I fell out of love with the Phillies for a time when Richie left the team," Jim said.

Jim Donahue continued to seek autographs of professional players as they played in Philadelphia. Besides Ashburn, Jim has the signatures of Robin Roberts and Sparky Anderson, who played second base for the Phillies in the late 1950's. "I played second base and I loved Sparky. The Phillies actually had two Andersons. Harry "The Horse" Anderson was an outfielder. My autograph books also contain the signature of Benny Bengough. He was a member of the feared 1927 Yankees and later he was a Phillies' coach. I used to see the Philadelphia Warriors play pro basketball and I also have the autographs of basketball legends Wilt Chamberlain and Elgin Baylor."

Jim's childhood autograph book has survived, saved by his mother, Mary. "Mom kept it all those years. When we were cleaning out the house in 2001 after her death, I found the books and the photographs Dad took that day."

* * *

The 45 seconds that star player Richie Ashburn spent with Jim Donahue on Saturday, July 20, 1957, was a significant event in the life of Jim Donahue. Those 45 seconds would also be a significant moment in the professional life of Richie "Whitey" Ashburn.

2

Tilden Years

RICHIE ASHBURN WAS a proud product of a small mid-western farming community. As he traveled through the major leagues and settled in the big city of Philadelphia, he never forgot his upbringing and his roots. When he departed Tilden, Nebraska, Richie didn't leave behind his mid-western wit, humor and charm.

* * *

During Richie's many years in the broadcast booth of the Philadelphia Phillies, he would joke with his longtime on-air partner Harry Kalas about the size of Tilden and the lack of red lights in the small town. Indeed, Tilden was then and has remained an American town embodying the joys of a simpler time.

The earliest settlers of the town near the Elkhorn River began arriving after the conclusion of the Civil War in 1868. The first name of the settlement was Burnett and it straddled the line dividing Madison and Antelope counties. The first official census counted 218 residents.

Burnett's residents were having a problem with their mail. The United States Post Office couldn't keep the letters and packages destined for Burnett's residents separate from the mail being sent to those in a town named Bennett. The federal government solved the dilemma by changing Burnett's name to Tilden in 1887. The town was named for New Yorker Samuel

J. Tilden who was the Democratic candidate for president in 1876. Tilden won the popular vote over Civil War General Rutherford B. Hayes but Hayes became the 19th President of the United States when he prevailed in a disputed Electoral College vote. Some of town's residents were slow to use the new name of Tilden and the town council had to enforce the name change by passing a city ordinance.

Early in the 20th century the town's population topped 1,000 people. The number of residents in Richie's home town has remained steady over the years as the 2000 census pegged the number of people calling Tilden home at 1,078. Even though the town's population has been small, it has produced two notable residents; Ashburn and L. Ron Hubbard, who was the founder of Scientology and a science fiction writer.

Today, Tilden is part of the Cowboy Trail, a section of the former Chicago and Northwestern Railroad that is being turned into the longest bicycling and hiking trail in the United States. Tilden hasn't forgotten one of its favorite sons as the town's website uses baseballs as icons. The town proudly states Hall of Fame baseball player Richie Ashburn's birthplace is Tilden and that the municipal baseball park was renamed Ashburn Field in his honor. Memorabilia of Richie Ashburn can also be seen at the Stewart Toy Museum on Main Street in Tilden, according to the website.

* * *

On March 19, 1927, Neil and Toots Ashburn became the proud parents of a set of twins. They named the brother and sister Don Richard and Donna Ruth Ashburn. Parents Neil and Toots had been married five years before the arrival of the twins. With the births of the twins, the number in the household increased to six as Neil and Toots already had two children, Bob and Bette. Neil and Toots decided to call young Don Richard by the name of Richie because of the similarities in twins' first names.

The family lived in a one-bedroom house with an outhouse serving as a bathroom. Life was not easy as the nation was entering the Great Depression and money was tight for many families across the land. The close-knit Ashburn family survived and prospered in the little town of Tilden.

Neil Ashburn worked with his father, Bob Ashburn, in the family blacksmith shop. Richie's mother Toots worked as a telephone operator for AT&T. Both parents changed careers during their lifetimes. Neil Ashburn later became a monument maker and many gravestones in the local cemetery were products of Neil's toil. Toots became a dietician.

Neil Ashburn turned to another activity to make some money for the family: baseball. He played second base for a local semi-professional team. Neil spent weekends traveling to games in neighboring communities. He was paid $25 per game, a sum that would sometimes surpass his weekly pay at his everyday job.

The love of baseball was thus instilled early in Richie Ashburn. Richie inherited his father's wit and his love of the national pastime. As a youngster, Richie took part in a number of sports, including basketball, tennis and swimming but baseball was his sport. His athletic ability was evident to anyone who watched him play any of the sports. Richie did forgo one sport, football. His family was worried that a football injury would dash any hopes of a professional baseball career for Richie.

One of those who knew early that Richie was a gifted athlete was his father. Neil Ashburn had visions of his son playing in the major leagues and guided Richie's youthful pursuits towards that end.

Richie's athleticism far exceeded what many expected from his physical appearance. As he participated in youth baseball in the area's midget baseball league, some opposing players made fun of Richie's size. Richie proved to those players and his teammates that his physical size didn't diminish his talent. Richie was dedicated to the sport and had a burning desire to succeed. Richie worked hard to become a superb catcher and earned national recognition playing American Legion baseball.

Neil Ashburn believed the quickest path to Major League Baseball for his son was to have Richie become a catcher. Richie was certainly fast enough to play any of the outfield positions but he was never going to be a slugger. Donning the protective catching gear, commonly called "the tools of ignorance at the time," was to be Richie's ticket to the major leagues. The disparaging term was used under the mistaken belief that only brawn and not brains was needed to be a catcher.

Richie Ashburn excelled as a catcher in the American Legion league and word soon spread throughout the major league scouting system that young Ashburn could be a major league caliber player. Richie was fast, sure-footed and fearless. He could hit and he could steal bases. He had the skills that could be honed into a professional player.

Richie's small physical build, especially for a catcher, troubled many of the professional scouts until he had a chance to perform at the Polo Grounds in New York City. Richie was selected to play on the West squad in the Esquire's All-American Boy's Baseball Game. The game was known throughout the land. During World War II, the game was even televised. Many notable major league players were connected with the contest. In 1945, a team coached by Babe Ruth defeated a team coached by another baseball great, Ty Cobb, by a score of 5-4.

Richie played before such greats as Connie Mack and Mel Ott. Ott was the manager for Richie's team and Richie later commented that he was disappointed that Ott didn't put him in the starting lineup. Richie impressed many of those watching him but not everyone. Richie told a story of meeting Branch Rickey. Rickey was an innovative baseball executive who was elected to the Hall of Fame in 1967. Rickey was known for being a very good judge of baseball talent. Richie recalls Rickey telling him it would be best if he returned to Nebraska and just did whatever he was going to do but not think about professional baseball as a career.

Richie ignored Rickey's advice.

Baseball scouts vied to sign Richie to a contract. The most aggressive teams pursuing Richie were the Cleveland Indians and the Chicago Cubs. The scout for the Indians was the first one to secure Richie's signature on a major league contract. Richie was 16 years old and still in high school at the time he received the contract in the mail from the Indians. Neil Ashburn advised his son not to sign but Richie wanted to play professional baseball and he decided become a Cleveland Indian player.

Neil Ashburn wasn't the only person unhappy with Richie's decision to sign a contract at the age of 16. Commissioner of Baseball Judge Kenesaw Landis also had reservations about having high school students becoming professional players. Judge Landis summoned young Richie and his father to his office in Chicago for a discussion.

Landis voided the contract and fined Cleveland $500 for signing the high school student. The message was clear to other major league clubs: stay away from high school players. Landis did allow Richie to keep the $1,000 signing bonus.

Richie was once again an amateur player being pursued by major league teams. The Cubs stayed in the hunt along with the Philadelphia Phillies. Young Ashburn's second contract was with the Chicago Cubs. By this time he had graduated from high school and was age eligible to be signed. Ashburn's second contract also had legal issues and it too was eventually voided.

Cubs scout Cy Slapnika was successful in getting Richie's signature on a contract and Ashburn was to play in Nashville.

One clause in the contract, ruled to be illegal, provided for Richie to share with the Nashville club in his purchase price if the Cubs decided to buy Richie's contract.

Richie was again a young and promising baseball player available to all major league teams. The third time proved to be the charm for both Richie Ashburn and the Philadelphia Phillies.

While waiting for his professional baseball career to begin, Richie attended Norfolk Junior College. Tilden and Norfolk, Nebraska, are neighboring towns connected by Route 275. The distance between the two towns is about 20 miles.

Phillies' scout Eddie Krajnik was successful in signing Richie Ashburn to a legitimate contract in 1945. That year Richie Ashburn began catching for the Utica Blue Sox minor league team. The first season of professional baseball resulted in a major change for Richie. He was switched from catcher to an outfielder.

Blue Sox manager Eddie Sawyer immediately recognized Ashburn's speed and his ability to contribute in the outfield. One often-repeated story about Ashburn demonstrated why his stint behind the plate was destined to be brief. Catchers are taught to run to first base on ground balls to the infield in case a throw eludes a first baseman. On one play Richie raced to first base and beat the batter to the bag. Sawyer, Richie's future major league manager, switched Richie's position to center field. The move would utilize Richie's speed and save a lot of wear and tear on the player's legs. Catchers are constantly up and down during a game and leg problems are common. Neil Ashburn was concerned that his son's path to the major leagues would be blocked if he was a centerfielder. Sawyer eventually convinced Neil Ashburn that the switch of positions was best for Richie.

In his first season of professional baseball, Richie also showed signs of his batting ability. He played in 106 games and compiled a .312 batting average. He led the team in stolen bases. Richie also was introduced to some of his future major league teammates, including Putsy Caballero, Granny Hamner and Stan Lopata.

Richie was set to build upon his outstanding first year as a professional baseball player but Uncle Sam had other ideas. World War II was in its final days when the United States Army drafted Richie. The war concluded before Richie saw active service but for more than a year Richie was away from professional baseball. He spent most of that time in Alaska handling mail duties.

The time away from baseball didn't diminish his skills. He returned to Utica for the 1947 season and had another outstanding year. At the plate he batted .362. He also stole 27 bases as his team went on to win the Eastern League championship.

Richie's path to the major leagues was clear. Philadelphia Phillies' manager Ben Chapman saw enough promise in the speedy outfielder to summon Richie to the 1948 Phillies' spring training camp in Clearwater, Florida.

Richie's baseball career was about to take him away from his beloved Tilden, Nebraska. He would return in the fall of 1948 and visit Norfolk Junior College. While there he met Herberta Cox. She was known as Herbie. The couple went to a movie and then had additional dates. Just about one year later Richie and Herbie were married on November 6, 1949, in Herbie's hometown of Battle Creek, Nebraska.

Whiz Kids

RICHIE ASHBURN'S FIRST major league spring training camp was in Clearwater, Florida. Phillies' manager Ben Chapman had invited Richie to train with his squad of major league players after being impressed with the speedy outfielder's performance in the minor leagues.

Richie's first year in a major league camp was also the first year the Phillies made Clearwater its spring training base. Richie's home away from home was in the Phoenix Hotel. He was assigned his first roommate, Robin Roberts. Roberts, one of the greatest right-handed pitchers in the history of the Philadelphia Phillies, was destined to have a Hall of Fame career. Richie and Roberts were both rookies during the 1948 season. They also had played together in the minor leagues.

The first year for Richie predated Carpenter Field, built in 1967. Carpenter Field updated the facilities available to Richie and his teammates in the 1940's and 1950's. Carpenter Field is still used in spring training by the Phillies' major league and minor league players. The Phillies teams in the Gulf Coast Rookie League and the Florida Instructional League also play at the stadium.

The Phillies continue to spend the spring training months of the season in Clearwater, close to the beaches of the Gulf of Mexico. The team now trains in the Bright House Networks Field complex.

* * *

Even though Chapman saw major league potential in Richie's abilities, Richie was not expected to make an immediate contribution to the team. A spot in the Phillies' starting lineup was blocked by Harry Walker.

Walker, an outfielder with tremendous bat control, had had an exceptional season with the Phillies in 1947. He played center field and hit for a .371 batting average after being traded from the St. Louis Cardinals. His combined average of .363 led the National League. Walker had begun his professional career with the Phillies organization. He was signed in 1937 but traded to the St. Louis Cardinals in 1940.

Walker, known as "Harry the Hat" for his habit of continually adjusting his cap between pitches, was also one of the stars of the Cardinals' 1946 World Series championship team. Walker had knocked in the winning run in the seventh game of the World Series. Walker's hit scored Enos Slaughter as the Cardinals defeated the Boston Red Sox for baseball's crown. During his eleven-year major league career, Walker had a batting average of .296.

With a World Series' hero and batting champ playing center field for the Phillies, Richie's chances of playing seemed slim as spring training began in 1948. Walker helped Richie secure the starting job by deciding he should receive a larger salary increase than the Phillies' officials were offering. He was a hold-out as the spring training began and Richie took over the position.

A preseason story in a Philadelphia paper by Frank Yeutter had a headline of: "Ashburn's skill poses outfield problem for Phils: Speed may earn Richie berth from seasoned flychasers." The story reported that coming into spring training camp Richie was "merely a name. . . . Coming into the training camp of a team that has a center fielder like Harry Walker, certainly wasn't a hopeful situation. That is, it would be to most guys, but not Richie."

At the time the story was written, Richie had started in five games and played nine innings while Walker was "nursing sore feet and shin splints." Richie had helped the Phillies defeat the New York Yankees that day. The story concluded, "It's unreasonable to expect a green kid to make the majors overnight but Mel Ott did it at 16 from the Louisiana sandlots."

With Walker busy negotiating his contract, the opportunity to play in spring training was all Richie needed to establish himself as a major league centerfielder. As Richie's playing time increased, Walker's playing time with the Phillies diminished. In 1947, Walker played 127 games in the outfield for Philadelphia and appeared in a total of 130 games. He also played first base. In 1948, Richie's rookie season, Walker's playing time dropped to 112 games.

Richie's swift ascent from playing in the minor leagues in Utica to being the Phillies' starting centerfielder must have come as a surprise to Walker. Despite batting .292 for the Phillies in 1948, Walker was traded to the Chicago Cubs for Bill Nicholson at the end of the season.

* * *

Richie Ashburn played in the first major league game he ever saw. His debut came on April 20, 1948, against the Boston Braves. Richie secured his first major league hit in his second at bat against Braves' pitcher Johnny Sain. Richie was just getting started. He would have 2,573 additional hits in his career.

Richie wrote a newspaper article recalling his first game. The story appeared in the *Philadelphia Daily News* in 1988. Richie wrote that manager Ben Chapman warned him that Sain was one of the best pitchers in the league. Richie agreed with Chapman's assessment of Sain's abilities. At the age of 21, he was living his dream, Richie wrote.

Richie played before an estimated 35,000 fans that April day in 1948. He stated he had never seen so many people in one place.

Richie dazzled the Philadelphia fans, his teammates and the baseball community his rookie season. He utilized his speed stealing 32 bases and leading the National League. His bat control made him difficult to strike out. He batted .333 for the year with 154 hits in 117 games.

A *Philadelphia Inquirer* sportswriter, Stan Baumgartner, called Ashburn the "Nebraska Comet."

His play resulted in a berth on the National League All-Star squad. He was the only rookie selected. He was named Rookie of the Year by *The Sporting News*. Stan Musial was named the Most Valuable Player in the National League in 1948 and Richie finished eleventh in the voting in his first season.

The All-Star game was played on July 13, 1948, in St. Louis. Richie played center field and had two hits in four at bats. He also stole a base and scored a run. His teammates included Ralph Kiner, Red Schoendienst, Stan Musial, Johnny Mize, Pee Wee Reese, Bobby Thompson and Johnny Sain, the pitcher who surrendered Richie's first major league hit. The American League team included Joe DiMaggio and Ted Williams. The American League defeated the National League, 5-2.

Richie would be named an All-Star squad member five times in his career.

Richie's on-the-field play was supported by his home environment during his rookie season. His parents, Neil and Toots Ashburn, decided to rent a house in Narberth, a suburb of the City of Philadelphia. During the season, Richie's parents looked after their son and also other young players, including Robin Roberts and Curt Simmons. All three were teammates at Utica. Toots Ashburn would cook meals and Neil Ashburn would talk baseball. After the season concluded, the Ashburn family returned to Tilden, Nebraska.

Harry Paxton of *The Saturday Evening Post* later wrote an article about the unique living arrangements. The story started, "That House Where the Ballplayers Live: Baseball has never known anything quite like this home in which Pa and Ma Ashburn—parents of the Phillies Richie—shepherd $100,000 worth of kids through the perils of a big-league career."

Paxton spent a day at the home and reported Charley Bicknell and Jack Mayo were also there with Richie, Roberts and Simmons. Paxton wrote Neil Ashburn liked to watch the games from the press box while his wife viewed them from the family section in the stands of Connie Mack Stadium.

The article reported that the "boys" would spend time talking about game and rehashing plays before going to bed. The story stated after a loss, the players would go straight to bed. The day Paxton visited the Dodgers defeated Roberts and the Phillies.

Another story by author Helen O. Mankin reported the consumption of "10 quarts of milk a day and eggs disappear by the dozen." Mankin wrote that "Mrs. Ashburn was a wonderful cook." The author also wrote the main topics of conversation were baseball and girls.

Richie was a success in his rookie season. His .333 batting average was second in the league to the legendary Stan Musial. As a team, the Phillies were less successful as Philadelphia finished sixth in the National League with a record of 66-88.

* * *

The 1949 season, Richie's second in the major leagues, was solid but not as spectacular as his rookie year. He batted .284 with 188 hits and stole nine bases. The team certainly improved, winning more games than it lost. The 81-73 record was good enough for third place in the National League.

The Phillies baseball fans were starved for a pennant. The franchise was established in 1883 and the team was initially known as the Quakers. Before the end of the decade the

Quakers became the Phillies. The Philadelphia franchise had a number of winning seasons during its early years but the team couldn't capture a championship. Early in the 20th century, the team suffered a number of losing seasons, including dropping 100 games in 1904. The Phillies record that year was 52-100.

The pennant drought for the Phillies ended in 1915, 33 years after the Phillies began playing major league baseball. Pitcher Grover Cleveland Alexander was the star of the pitching staff, winning 31 games. He tossed four, one-hit games during the season. The Phillies' big slugger that year was Gavvy Cravath, who set league records with 24 home runs. Five years later Babe Ruth would break Cravath's record.

The Phillies met the Boston Red Sox in the 1915 World Series. The first game went to the Phillies as Alexander out-pitched the Boston ace, Ernie Shore. The Phillies went on to lose the next three games by the identical scores of 2-1. The Phillies lost the fifth game of the series, and the World Series, as the Red Sox Harry Hooper hit a home run in the ninth inning to ensure a Red Sox win.

In 1916, the Phillies came within three games of winning another pennant but the Brooklyn Dodgers prevailed. Another pennant drought began for the team and fans. Losing seasons for the Phillies were common occurrences during the next three decades. For the years 1943 and 1944 the Phillies exchanged their red uniforms for predominately blue ones and were called the Blue Jays. The new look didn't help the team to win as both seasons resulted in at least 90 losses. By 1945 the red uniforms were back and so were the Phillies.

As the 1950 season commenced, the Phillies were searching for their second league championship. In 1949, the Phillies posted its first winning record in 17 seasons. The fans were ready for a run at the pennant.

The 1950 team did win the National League championship. The team was known as The Whiz Kids as the core members were made up of players developed in the Phillies' farm system. Richie, Robin Roberts, Del Ennis, Granny Hamner, Willie Jones and Curt Simmons were young and exciting players. Team owners added some experienced veterans to the squad to aid the youngsters.

Richie had another spectacular year in 1950. His batting average once again soared above the .300 mark as he hit .303. He led the league in triples with 14, he had 180 hits and he also stole 14 bases. Richie was also developing into one of the premier defensive centerfielders of all time. He handled 418 chances in 1950 and committed only five errors. He also had eight outfield assists despite what many believed was a subpar throwing arm. His arm and his defense played a major role in the Phillies attaining the World Series in 1950.

For a majority of the season, the Phillies were in first place. With just eleven games remaining in the regular season, the Phillies were leading the league by seven games. The advantage quickly evaporated as the Phillies lost eight of the next ten games. The Phillies entered the last day of the regular season with a one-game lead. The team needed to defeat the second place Brooklyn Dodgers at Ebbets Field, New York, to avoid entering a playoff.

On Sunday, October 1, 1950, as expected, Phillies' ace Robin Roberts was on the mound for the team. He faced Dodger great Don Newcombe. Each pitcher had won 19 games during the regular season. New York fans - 35,073 was the official attendance - jammed the stands for the season finale. The game was scoreless until the sixth inning when Dick Sisler scored a run for the Phillies. A Dodger homer in the bottom of the inning tied the score.

The game remained 1-1 as the bottom of the ninth inning began. A run for the Dodgers and the two teams would be tied in the standings. The Dodgers' first two batters reached base. With runners on first and second, Duke Snider came to bat against Roberts. Snider lined a hard single to center and Cal Abrams, the runner on second, tried to score. Ashburn fired a strike to Phillies' catcher Stan Lopata and Abrams was out by ten feet, according to some observers of the game.

Richie's play became legendary in the annals of Philadelphia Phillies' baseball as the throw thwarted a Brooklyn victory.

"My throw to nail Abrams has been cussed and discussed for years," Richie wrote in a September 27, 1990, article for the *Philadelphia Daily News*. "The truth is, I had shortened my position in center field a few steps as every outfielder would do with the winning run on second base in the bottom of the ninth. Snider hit a bullet, a perfect one-hopper; and all I had to do was get off a decent throw to home. To be accurate, it was a fairly routine play executed perfectly in a very crucial situation."

The Phillies were still in danger of losing the game after Richie's throw to nail Abrams. Jackie Robinson was next batter for the Dodgers, but Roberts walked him and then retired Carl Furillo and Gil Hodges to end the inning.

In the tenth inning, Eddie Waitkus and Richie were on base with one out. First baseman Waitkus almost didn't play for the Phillies in 1950. The previous season he was shot by 19-year-old Ruth Steinhagen at Chicago's Edgewater Beach Hotel. Steinhagen was placed in a mental hospital and Waitkus recovered from the June 15, 1949, incident to play major league baseball.

Dick Sisler earned his place in Phillies' history in the tenth inning as he hit a clutch home run to put the Phillies in the lead, 4-1, as Richie and Waitkus scored ahead of Sisler. Roberts set down the Dodgers in the bottom of the tenth for a complete game victory. Roberts earned his 20th win of the season and the Phillies had the second National League crown in franchise history.

The Phillies faced another New York opponent in the 1950 World Series. The defending world champion New York Yankees opposed The Whiz Kids.

Because Roberts pitched against Brooklyn, he was unavailable to throw the first game of the series against the Yankees. Another of the Phillies' best starting pitchers, Curt Simmons, was unavailable because late in the season he was summoned to the military. Manager Eddie Sawyer decided that his top relief pitcher, Jim Konstanty, would start the first game. Konstanty pitched strictly in relief and compiled a 16-7 record with a 2.66 earned run average during the regular season. Konstanty fooled the Yankees for most of the afternoon and in eight innings he allowed only one run and four hits. The superb effort wasn't enough as Vic Raschi tossed a two-hit shutout for the Yankees. Richie was hitless in four attempts in his first World Series game.

Roberts was rested and ready to throw the second game of the series for the Phillies. He battled the Yankees' Allie Reynolds in a pitching duel. The game was tied 1-1 after nine innings. Richie had two hits for the game and drove in the only Phillies' run. Joe DiMaggio won the game in the tenth inning with a home run.

The Phillies received another fine game from a starting pitcher in the third game of the series from Ken Heintzelman. Heintzelman and the Phillies were leading 2-1 after seven innings. With two outs in the eighth inning, Heintzelman walked three batters to load the bases. Sawyer switched pitchers and Konstanty, the opening game starter, was again on the mound for the Phillies. An error allowed the tying run to score before the third out was recorded. The Yankees scored another run in the ninth for a 3-2 victory. Richie contributed one hit to the Phillies' offense.

A rookie took the mound for Casey Stengel's Yankees in game four. The rookie, Ed "Whitey" Ford, was the winning pitcher as the Phillies lost the game 5-2 and the series, four games to none.

As for the Phillies' Richie "Whitey" Ashburn, he was hitless against the Yankee's Whitey Ford. For the series, Richie had three hits in 17 plate appearances for a .176 batting average. He had one double and one RBI. The four games he played would constitute his only appearances in a World Series.

The Whiz Kids earned a place in the hearts of the baseball fans of Philadelphia even though the team lost the World Series to the New York Yankees. Today, they are fondly recalled and are remembered for their youth, spirit and hustle.

Richie Ashburn was one of the key members of The Whiz Kids and would remain forever a fan favorite.

The Amazing Mets

RICHIE ASHBURN'S PERFORMANCE during the 1950 championship established him as one of the emerging stars of the National League. Richie's rocket-like speed, his magic manipulating a bat and his fierce competitiveness were showcased during the World Series.

Richie's midwest charm also led to a number of national product endorsements. In a television commercial for Gillette, he was called a "flashy young outfielder for the Phillies." In a radio commercial for Wheaties, he is called a "fleet-footed outfielder" who "fires up with Wheaties."

Richie was the type of player that Philadelphia fans love. He played the game hard, the way it should be played. He was a fierce competitor. He didn't like to lose and he never tolerated those who didn't give a maximum effort.

He also didn't think much of pitchers or at least said so while a broadcaster. Richie often said he wouldn't want his daughter to marry one. Richie believed he should never make an out. He claimed pitchers cheated and was known to yell at them during a game.

Another trait that endeared Richie to the Phillies' fans was his humor. He was funny and he was gracious. He mingled with the fans and he gave freely of his time to sign autographs. Richie connected with the fans of Philadelphia and the fans of Philadelphia accepted Richie as an adopted son.

Philadelphia is known as a town that is tough on its athletes, even star players. Richie "Whitey" Ashburn was the exception. During a nationally televised baseball game in 2010, former major league player and television announcer Tim McCarver called Richie Ashburn the most beloved athlete in Philadelphia's history.

* * *

While Richie compiled impressive statistics on the field during the 1950's, The Whiz Kids never repeated their championship season. In fact, a year after appearing in the World Series against the New York Yankees, the Phillies failed to even compile a winning record. The team finished in fifth place in the league and won 73 of 154 games.

The Phillies improved the following two seasons and once again won more games than they lost. The improvement wasn't nearly enough to compete for a league crown. The remaining years of the decade were spent in the second division of the National League. They were bleak years for the fans of the team. In 1958 and 1959, the Phillies finished dead last in the National League.

* * *

While the Phillies were having difficulty winning games, Richie was being noticed by the national media. *Sports Illustrated* printed a long article in May 1953 about Richie with a number of illustrations of Richie demonstrating the proper way to play the outfield, run the bases, steal bases and slide.

The Saturday Evening Post profiled Richie in a story on March 10, 1956, by Harry T. Paxon. The article began by saying Richie led his league in batting and was also the champ at throwing out runners. The story also said Richie consistently gets on base more often than any other player.

The article states, "For eight seasons now Ashburn has been delivering base hits in remarkable quantity. He covers as much ground in the outfield as any of the more glamorized fly chasers. He is one of the faster men on the bases. Yet it wasn't until last year, when he won the National League batting championship, that many people began to appreciate just how good he is.

"Richie is by no means a shy or retiring personality. On or off the field, if anyone barks at him, he barks right back. . . . Folks in Richie's home area in Nebraska can testify to the unflagging determination with which he just pursued baseball success since boyhood." The article quotes Richie's father as saying, "I knew Richie was going to be good almost from the time he could walk. He was so springy and quick in his movements."

Talking about his dip in offensive production after his rookie year, Richie told the writer, "It was my own fault. I reported to spring training with a swelled head and a big-shot attitude, which resulted in my learning very little, and not listening to people I should have, and thinking that baseball was just a little easier than it was."

The story also talked about Richie's wife. "Herbie is brown-haired, attractive and highly personable." The story said the couple met when Herbie was studying to be a teacher. She had never seen a baseball game before seeing Richie play in the 1948 All-Star game in St. Louis.

Richie listened to the advice given by his father. One Associated Press story in 1949 has Richie giving him credit for advice on the first home run he hit out of the park. The pitcher was Carl Erskine. At the time Richie had two inside-the-park home runs. "Dad said, 'Kid, they don't pay off in this game for bunts and beating out infield hits. You have to drive in runs and hit the long ball. Drop those hands to the end of the bat and pull for the fences. You'll help both yourself and the club.' Pop Ashburn kept after the kid all spring and Richie showed signs of taking the advice. He socked two home runs in one game in Florida. Pop Ashburn said, 'That's my boy,' when Richie hit the home run."

* * *

The team was mired in mediocrity, a state it wouldn't escape until the end of the 1970's. The Phillies did have some exciting players for the fans to watch during the 1950's. The top two leaders on the team were pitcher Robin Roberts and outfielder Richie Ashburn.

The year after winning the National League crown, Richie was once again an All-Star and he finished seventh in voting for the league's Most Valuable Player. During one double-header, he collected eight hits in ten at bats, a record that still stands for the Phillies for most hits in a doubleheader. He led the league with 221 hits and finished second in the league in batting with a .344 average. In the All-Star game, he collected two hits and scored two runs in a National League victory.

Robin Roberts joined Richie as an All-Star in 1953. Roberts was the starting pitcher for the National League while Richie drove in a run with a base hit in his only plate appearance.

Pitchers had major problems trying to retire Richie. At the plate, Richie would foul off pitches and wait out walks. In 1954, those abilities allowed him to lead the National League in walks with 125 and gave him the best on-base percentage at .441.

The best example of Richie's ability to foul off pitch after pitch was an oft told tale of a game against the New York Giants in 1957. Alice Roth, the wife of a sports writer for the *Philadelphia Bulletin*, was in the stands that day. Twice in the same at bat, Richie hit the woman with foul balls. The first one broke her nose. While medical personnel were taking her from the stands, Richie kept batting and fouling off pitches. A second foul ball hit the woman.

Another story Richie told concerned a player who asked him to hit his wife who was in the stands during a game. Richie wasn't attempting to hit the woman but one ball came close. The player reportedly told Richie if Richie could hit the next foul ball two rows over from the spot where he landed the last one, Richie would hit his wife.

Richie's ability to collect base hits and hit for a high batting average continued. In 1955, he won his first of two National League batting crowns with a .338 average. His on-base percentage was .449, also leading the National League. Richie followed up his batting title with a .303 average the next year. In 1957, his average dropped a few points to .297.

In 1958, Richie had a banner year for the Phillies. He earned his second National League batting crown with a .350 average. He also led the league in hits with 215, triples with 13 and walks with 97. His on-base percentage was also number one in the league at .440. He swiped 30 bases.

Richie's play was worthy of another trip to the All-Star game and he was selected as an alternate. A number of National League teams had great centerfielders during the 1950's. The starting centerfielder that year was Willie Mays.

Richie believed he played in the best era for baseball since it was post-segregation and all players were eligible to compete and before the league expanded and added teams. The added teams diluted the talent.

Richie Ashburn was an elite player in baseball's golden era.

As the Phillies remained mired in the bottom of the National League, Ashburn continued to produce at a high level. His final season as a member of the Phillies wasn't as productive as his previous years, but he still had a solid year. He batted .266, the lowest average of his career as a starting player, with 150 hits and 79 walks.

* * *

When the 1959 season came to an end, rumors began circulating in the press that Richie's time in Philadelphia was at an end. A fine twelve-year career in Philadelphia was about to conclude. Richie gave interviews to reporters saying if he could no longer play in Philadelphia, he would like to play closer to his home in Tilden, Nebraska.

Richie got his wish as the Phillies traded him to the Chicago Cubs. On January 11, 1960, the Phillies shipped Richie to the Cubs for pitcher John Buzhardt and infielders Al Dark and Jim Woods.

Richie didn't change his style as a Cub. He was a good teammate and he was a fierce competitor. In his first season with Chicago, he led the league in walks with 116 and on-base percentage with .415. His average improved to .291 and he had 159 hits.

His production and playing time diminished in his second year with Chicago. He was called upon to play in 109 games and gathered 79 hits. His batting average dipped to .257.

* * *

Major League Baseball was ready for expansion. The game was healthy. Fans across the country wanted their cities to have their own teams. The National League also wanted to have a representative in New York City and New York wanted a team. Years earlier the New York Giants and Brooklyn Dodgers left New York for new homes in California.

New York City Mayor Robert F. Wagner appointed a committee in 1957 to explore the possibility of securing another team for New York. The members were former postmaster general James Farley, attorney Bill Shea, and businessmen Clint Blume and Bernard Gimbel. On October 17, 1960, the Mets franchise was formally awarded by the National League to a group headed by Joan Payson. On March 6, 1961, The

New York Metropolitan Baseball Club Inc., formally received a certificate of membership from National League President Warren Giles.

A second expansion team was formed and named the Houston Colt .45's.

The New York Mets needed players and on October 10, 1961, the first expansion draft in National League history took place. At the Netherland-Hilton Hotel in Cincinnati, Mets officials selected 22 players from other teams and spent $1.8 million dollars.

One National League player destined to become an original Met was Richie "Whitey" Ashburn of the Chicago Cubs. In 1962, Ashburn played for the legendary Casey Stengel, the manager who guided the New York Yankees to a World Series victory over The Whiz Kids in 1950.

One newspaper reported on the selection of Richie, "The New York Mets yesterday acquired another slightly aged though still highly capable player they expect to give their club stability when it makes its debut in the National League next year.

Richie had some well-known teammates on the 1962 Mets. Frank Thomas, Marv Thornberry and Choo Choo Colemen played on the team along with Roger Craig and Don Zimmer.

Before the season began, Richie recalled they were all treated as heroes. The original Mets wouldn't be considered heroes by the time the season ended. The team had charm, if not ability. They would be remembered as lovable losers. The Mets would be on the wrong end of a score in more games in one season than any other team in Major League Baseball history.

The Mets played the franchise's first game in St. Louis against the Cardinals on April 11, 1962. They were scheduled to play a day earlier but rain cancelled the contest. The Mets lost 11-4. Richie played center field and batted lead off. He had one hit in five at bats. In the Mets home opener at the Polo

Grounds on April 13, 1962, the Mets played the Pittsburgh Pirates and lost 4-3.

Being the leadoff batter, Richie was the first player for the Mets ever to bat in a game. He also scored the first run in Mets' history, scoring in third inning of the first game against St. Louis.

The first victory came on April 23 as the Mets defeated Pittsburgh by a score of 9-1. Richie sat out the first Mets victory as Jim Hickman was the centerfielder. Jay Hook was the winning pitcher for New York.

For the year, the Mets ended up with a record of 40 wins and 120 losses and finished tenth, dead last in the National League. The team seemed to invent new ways to lose games. One story Richie told involved Elio Chacon, the Mets' shortstop, and outfielder Frank Thomas. Chacon didn't understand English and Richie and Chacon had a tendency to collide while trying to catch shallow fly balls. One day Richie called out in Spanish that he would catch the ball. Chacon avoided a collision with Richie but not Thomas. Thomas didn't understand Spanish.

When the Mets' inaugural season concluded, the team was 60 games behind the National League leader, the San Francisco Giants. The Giants' record was 103-62. Teammate Don Zimmer recalled that Richie's final offensive play as a Met was being part of a triple play.

The final game of the season was played on September 30, 1962, at Wrigley Field in Chicago. Only 3,960 fans were on hand to see Richie play his last game as a major league player. Richie started at second base and was credited with four assists and four putouts. He also committed an error, his sixth of the season. The Mets committed three in the game as the team lost 5-1.

At the plate, Richie had one single in four plate appearances. The hit came in his last at bat against Chicago pitcher Bob Buhl in the eighth inning. Richie and Sammy Drake were on base as Joe Pignatano stepped into the batter's box. Pignatano hit a fly ball that Cub second baseman Ken Hubbs tracked down for the first out of the play. Hubbs threw the ball to Ernie Banks at first base and Richie was the second out of the play. Banks' throw to shortstop Andre Rodgers concluded the triple play as Drake was called out.

At the age of 35, Richie had a solid year with the Mets. He played in 135 games and gathered 119 hits and stole 12 bases. He batted .306 and was once again an All-Star. Starting in center field that year for the National League was Willie Mays. Richie didn't participate in the All-Star contest.

Richie summed up his year with the Mets by joking that he was the best player on the worst team in Major League Baseball history.

Playing professional baseball for more than 15 years didn't dampen Richie's competitive spirit. During his almost 10,000 plate appearances, he never liked to make an out. He certainly didn't like to lose baseball games, especially more than 100 in one season.

With the prospect of another losing year ahead of him as a member of the New York Mets, Richie Ashburn decided to retire from baseball. One newspaper reported, "Richie Ashburn, one of the few bright spots in Casey Stengel's menagerie known as the Mets, is quitting baseball."

5

A Second Career

Richie Ashburn was a star during baseball's golden era. The decade of the 1950's was a time when all players, regardless of color, could compete. Major League Baseball was no longer segregated. The league had also not expanded, thus with fewer teams there were fewer major league players. Only the best-of-the best ballplayers were major leaguers.

Richie's career statistics are impressive. During his 15 seasons in the National League, Richie's batting average was .308. He won two batting titles and twice led the league in triples and once in stolen bases. Five times he was selected as a member of the National League All-Star team. For six straight seasons, Richie had the best batting average of the Phillies.

As a lead-off hitter, Richie had the perfect mix of skills. He was fast, he had bat control, he could bunt and he had an excellent batting eye for telling strikes from balls. Four times he led the league in on-base percentage, a title coveted by lead-off hitters. Lead-off hitters are paid to get on base and score on hits by the team's power hitters. For his career, Richie was on base almost four out of ten times he went to the plate. Four years Richie's on-base percentage was above .400. He drew 1,198 bases on balls and he scored 1,322 runs. During two seasons he scored more than 100 runs. His hit total was 2,574.

Richie was also durable. He played in 2,189 games during his Major League career. He made 9,736 plate appearances and was credited with 8,365 at bats. He walked 1,189 times. When Richie was on base, he was a threat to steal. He amassed 234 stolen bases in his career.

Defensively, Richie was one of the top outfielders in the league. His career fielding percentage was .983. In 6,377 chances, he made only 110 errors. His arm might not have been as powerful as other centerfielders, but he still collected 178 assists. He led National League outfielders in assists in 1952 with 23 and the next year with 18. He was also the league leader in 1957. Richie is ranked eighth in Phillies history in the category.

A power hitter Richie was not. His home run total for his career was 29 and seven of those were inside-the-park home runs. The most home runs he hit in one year took place during the last year his career. He hit seven with the New York Mets.

The lack of home runs hurt Richie's overall national popularity during his career. Star centerfielders able to knock the ball out of the park were featured in the major leagues at the time. The ones gaining the most attention were Mickey Mantle, Willie Mays and Duke Snider. All three played in New York City, where the national media loved them. While the three gained notoriety for their slugging, the one with the most hits for the 1950's was none other than Richie "Whitey" Ashburn.

Richie also didn't draw as much national attention as Mantle, Mays and Snider because he didn't appear in as many World Series as the trio. Mantle was in the Fall Classic a dozen times while Snider made it to the World Series six times and Mays made four appearances. The 1950 trip to the World Series with The Whiz Kids was the only time Richie was in the World Series.

Today, Richie Ashburn still holds the Philadelphia Phillies record for the most singles ever by a Phillies' player with 1,811. The Phillies 2010 Media Guide also lists Richie among the team leaders in a number of categories.

Many of the Phillies' batting records are held by Hall of Fame member Mike Schmidt. Richie ranks second in hits, games played and at bats, behind Schmidt. Richie has scored the third most runs in Phillies' history and is in the team's top ten in doubles, triples, total bases, walks, batting average, and on-base percentage.

As for single-season Phillies records, Ashburn ranks in the top 10 for hits, singles, walks, on-base percentage and batting average. Twice he had more than 100 walks in a season and was the league leader in 1954 with 125 bases on balls.

As Richie was quoted as saying, "I think I made the most of what I had in terms of ability. So, I have no regrets about my major league career."

On July 18, 1956, National League President Warren Giles called Ashburn "one of the most underrated players in baseball. Ashburn ranks with the best." Giles made the comment while awarding Richie a silver bat for winning the National League batting crown.

Baseball star George Sisler was quoted as saying, "In 30 years of big league baseball, I never saw better."

One question remained concerning Richie's career. Would the baseball writers association deem Richie's career worthy of the Hall of Fame?

* * *

To gain entrance to baseball's hallowed hall, a player must be selected by the Baseball Writers' Association of America. The board of directors of the National Baseball Hall of Fame and Museum, Inc., designated the writers as the election body. One election is held each year by active and honorary members of the writers' association. To be eligible, a writer needs to have covered baseball for at least ten years.

Players are eligible for consideration once they have been retired for five years. They then have a 15-year window to be considered by the writers. There are exceptions to the rules when a player dies. The writers are to consider a player's record, playing ability, integrity, sportsmanship, character and contributions to his teams.

A screening committee of the baseball writers' association prepares a ballot of those who have received votes on at least five percent of the ballots in the preceding election or are eligible for the first time and nominated by at least two of the six members of the screening committee. The ballots are to be ready by January 15 of each year and writers have 20 days to return ballots.

Write-in votes are not allowed and a writer can vote for a maximum of ten players on a ballot. Any player receiving at least 75 percent of the ballots cast is elected to the Hall of Fame.

* * *

Richie Ashburn had five years to wait before his first opportunity to be elected to the Hall of Fame. He was ready for his second career.

Richie's retirement as a player also gave him time to spend with his family. Richie and Herbie had six children during his playing days. The children were born during the baseball season when Richie was playing. He was not home for any of the births of his children. At times he used a baseball batting term to describe his absence. He said he was a miserable 0 for 6. Richie gave credit to his wife for helping his career and taking a leading role in raising their children. Richie spent time with his family and when the Phillies were home he always ate at least one meal with them. In the off-season, the family would spend time together at their home in Tilden.

The family included daughters Jean, Jan, Sue and Karen and sons Richard and John. Young Richard Ashburn's middle name is Evan, named after Ashburn's friend and Hall of Fame pitcher Robin Evans Roberts.

* * *

One of Richie's ideas for a second career was politics. He considered a run for Congress from Nebraska after hanging up his spikes. As early as 1958, Richie was quoted as saying politics might be in his future. Richie's political career never had a chance to materialize. The Phillies wanted Richie to return to Philadelphia as a broadcaster.

When first approached about calling the Phillies' games from behind a microphone, Ashburn declined to take the job. The Phillies told Richie to take some time to think about a broadcasting career. The Phillies would be back in touch with him before spring training began.

Richie also had the option of returning to the Mets as a player. George Weiss, the Mets' General Manager, offered Richie a raise but the money didn't tempt Richie to rejoin the Mets. "I wouldn't have missed the 1962 season for anything but I wouldn't want to go through it again," Richie wrote in an article in the *Philadelphia Daily News.*

As the spring training season approached, Richie admitted getting an itch to get back to baseball. As the Phillies were gathering in Clearwater, Florida, for the 1963 season, Richie was heading back to Clearwater for another rookie season, this time behind a microphone and in front of a television camera.

His broadcasting mentor and advisor was Bill Campbell, a long-time Phillies' broadcaster. Joining Richie and Campbell in the booth was Bryum Saam, another broadcasting veteran. Richie's broadcasting style was no different than his personal style. He was friendly and witty. His knowledge of the game came through loud and clear to the fans during the broadcasts.

Richie wasn't a natural broadcaster and he admitted that it took some time for him to be comfortable behind microphones and television cameras. Fans took to Richie from the beginning of his stint in the booth. Phillies' sponsors also grew to like Richie and overcame a few initial doubts.

A newspaper story reported, "Ashburn's practical ball yard knowledge melds with Saam and Campbell to give the Phils a touch of broadcasting class they have long needed. It is hoped Ashburn does not lose his natural appeal and be sucked into the circus-barker style that most baseball announcers use."

* * *

On January 8, 1963, George Vecsey of the *New York Times* wrote about Richie entering the broadcasting booth. The story stated, "Richie Ashburn won't run into any walls broadcasting Philadelphia Phillies games. That's only fitting for a man who's going to be 36 and has started thinking about security.

"But Ashburn ran into a wall when he was still 35 and still a baseball player. He did it for a 10th-place team, the New York Mets, and he'd do it again next season—if he weren't thinking about security."

"Ashburn said, 'I'd rather be on a playing field. There's no doubt about it. If it was any other job in any other city, I don't think I would have taken it. But this is a pretty good job, I could be carrying a lunch pail.' You like to go where people like you. He was cheered as loudly as any Phillie last year while a visitor.

"He needled all the Mets, particularly the lazy ones, and there were some. He threw bats at the shins of the scrubs who stayed in the batting cage too long. 'I loved New York.' He said he was well treated.

"(A broadcasting executive) said, 'He's a friendly guy, He's very popular in Philadelphia and he has a good sense of humor.' Ashburn said, 'I'm not sure I'm doing the right thing. But I had to quit sometime. I don't know. If a guy is fortunate enough to be able to play baseball maybe he should play until he can't do it any more.'"

In September of the previous year Ashburn, while with the Mets, did crash into a wall in Pittsburgh and briefly lost his memory. The incident took place during the fifth inning of the first game of a Labor Day doubleheader. Richie was chasing a ball hit by Bill Mazeroski when he fell in the Mets' bull pen. Richie remained in the game but later said he didn't remember the outcome and the fact that the Mets had lost the game. He didn't play the second game. Pittsburgh was also the scene of another injury as Richie broke a bone in his left hand while sliding in 1948, according to a United Press International report.

A *Philadelphia Bulletin* newspaper story reported on the same day that the Vecsey article appeared, "Putt-Putt to hang up glove." The writer attributed Richie's putt-putt nickname to the way he ran down the first base line. Another version has the baseball great Ted Williams giving Ashburn the nickname. Williams is quoted as saying, "That guy don't run, he's got an engine in the seat of his pants. He ought to go putt-putt when he runs."

While running track in Tilden he was once clocked at 0:09.9 in a 100-yard dash.

Williams also commented that Richie was always the first one dressed and on the field during his playing days.

* * *

The on-field fortunes of the Phillies didn't improve during the 1960's as Richie called the games from the booth. In 1964, the team made an unexpected run for the National League title and had a 6 ½ game lead with just twelve games remaining in the season. The team lost the lead. The collapse remains legendary in the history of Philadelphia sports.

The Phillies spent the rest of the decade without mounting a serious challenge for another crown. Richie spent the years improving his broadcasting style. The 1970 season was the final one for old Connie Mack Stadium. The Phillies were ready for the new Veterans Stadium constructed in South Philadelphia.

Besides the new broadcasting booth in the new stadium, Richie was to have a new broadcasting partner, Harry Kalas. The venerable Bill Campbell was at the end of his play-by-play career and the Phillies wanted a new voice to usher in the new stadium. They found Kalas in Houston and made him an offer he couldn't refuse.

The Phillies fans had a new voice and Richie had a new best friend, Harry Kalas. The personalities of Harry and Richie perfectly meshed and there was little doubt to the thousands that listened to the pair each night that they were close friends. Kalas was a professional broadcaster and Richie was a baseball expert. They made a perfect broadcasting team.

Richie's knowledge of the game almost led to his being called back to uniform as a Phillies' manager. A rumor swept the Phillies fan base that Richie wanted to take over the helm of the Phillies. Richie helped to fuel the rumor with comments made during broadcasts. Kalas was never sure if Richie was serious about becoming a manager. Also, the Phillies' team officials weren't sure if having Richie as a manager was a good idea. After all, no manager lasted forever, and one day a Phillies' official would have to fire Richie, the most loved athlete in Philadelphia.

While broadcasting, Richie decided to take on a second job. He became a sportswriter for the *Philadelphia Bulletin*. It was a Philadelphia institution for years but had started to fall into decline. The paper was first published in 1847 and ceased publication in 1982. The *Bulletin* has since been resurrected.

Richie worked hard on his columns and turned down a suggestion that a ghostwriter would pen his columns. Richie was a good writer and had many fans of his written work.

During the late 1970's and into 1980, the Phillies became a contending team. They made the playoffs three straight years, beginning in 1976. The first year the team lost the National League Championship series to the Cincinnati Reds as the

Reds swept all three games. The Phillies were back the next year but lost three of four to the Los Angeles Dodgers. In 1978, the Phillies had a rematch with the Dodgers. Again, the Phillies lost three of four games to Los Angeles.

The Phillies didn't make the playoffs in 1979 but did so in 1980. In one of the most exciting series in the history of baseball, certainly Phillies' baseball, the Phillies defeated the Houston Astros to win the National League title. The Phillies defeated the Astros 3 games to 2 games to face the Kansas City Royals in the World Series.

The Phillies' World Series drought came to an end on October 21, 1980, as Hall of Fame Phillies' pitcher Steve Carlton was the winner in game six. Tug McGraw saved the game and the Phillies were world champions for the first time in history.

Richie and Kalas didn't have an opportunity to broadcast the World Series for the Phillies and the team's fans. A Major League Baseball rule allowed only network announcers to broadcast the games. The rule was changed the next year after the Phillies' fans protested. The fans wanted to hear Richie and Kalas call the Phillies playoff games.

The changing of the major league baseball broadcasting rules was not the last time a rule would be challenged to right a wrong that slighted Richie.

6

No Hall Support

FAMILIES ACROSS THE Delaware Valley shared a favored relation. He was Richie Ashburn. Fans considered him part of their families. Almost every evening, Richie could either be heard on the radios in kitchens or seen and heard on the televisions in living rooms. Even though Richie no longer wore the # 1 uniform of the Phillies, he continued to be a fans' favorite in Philadelphia.

Richie never lost his passion for the game. When a pitcher wasn't terribly effective, Richie would tell his broadcasting partners that even at his age he could go down to the field, grab a bat and get three hits off the struggling thrower. When players weren't performing up to his standards, Richie was known to toss his hat in disgust and not so diplomatically tell his listeners that the offending player wasn't earning his keep.

Richie and Harry Kalas enjoyed themselves in the broadcasting booth. Richie would smoke his pipe during the broadcasts and wear a hat and sunglasses. The two announcers would never go hungry. A mere mention of a craving for a particular food would result in adoring fans delivering the requested fare to the broadcasters. They received pizza, hometown Tastykakes and various varieties of homemade goodies.

Broadcasting partner Chris Wheeler recalled one famous story about Richie and food. "One of our favorite places was a local pizzeria on Packer Avenue near the ballpark called Celebre's. They made the best pizza imaginable, and would frequently surprise us with a delivery at just the time, late in the game, when the free food from the press box was depleted and our stomachs were beginning to growl," Wheeler said. "On other occasions, irrepressible Whitey would make an announcement over the air that we'd like some pizza, even naming the toppings. Sure enough, about a half-hour later, an unmistakable smell would come from the back of the booth as a guy walked in carrying at least two large pies from our favorite place. Whitey would tell one of us to pay the tip, and he'd be back at the mike, thanking Ronnie and the guys from Celebre's for the delivery.

"Then one day (the Phillies' marketing department) informed us that the Phillies had made a deal with a major pizza sponsor, and the plugs for Celebre's would have to stop. Whitey didn't pay much attention to the edicts of people in authority, but at least he tried to abide by this one. However, one night we were involved in a late, rain-delayed game, there was no food on the counter behind us, and the thought of a Celebre's pie was on our minds. Between innings Whitey hatched a plot that was pure Ashburn.

"When we came back on the air, my part of the scam was to remind him that we had a special announcement to make. We always noted birthdays, anniversaries, special events, groups of fans at the game, and the like. So between pitches, I said to Whitey, 'Well, I know there's a birthday that you almost forgot to bring up because this has been such a long night.' 'That's right, Wheels,' he replied. 'We'd like to send our best wishers to the Celebre's twins, celebrating a birthday today. Happy Birthday, Plain and Pepperoni!' When he asked me how old they were, I managed to say, 'I hope about 20 minutes,' and then pretty much lost it. I had to lean back to keep my own laughter contained, while others retained their composure by leaving the booth, but Richie Ashburn just chuckled as he returned to the mike. And yes, less than half an hour later, two beautiful boxes arrived. This time we got the birthday gifts, in the form of plain and pepperoni."

* * *

After retiring from the game as a player, Richie remained physically active. He played squash, tennis and golf with fellow broadcasters, friends and active players. He was known to best many younger opponents on the tennis and squash courts. Preparing to putt on a golfing green with a cigar clenched in his mouth, he would tell those golfing with him, "Boys, this is a lock." Sometimes he would make the putt and sometimes he would not. He also joined his friends in card games.

Some seasons the Phillies played great baseball and other seasons they played poorly. Richie was always on top of his game. Listening to a game broadcast by Richie was lively and fun for the fans. Richie also taught many young fans the game of baseball and how it should be played. As with all broadcasters, at times a wrong name or fact would slip into the broadcast. When Richie was told of a mistake, he would say, "Boys, I just want to see if you were paying attention." When he used an improper first name, he would joke about the error by telling his broadcasting partners the name Richie misused was actually the name the misidentified player's best friends used.

* * *

While Richie succeeded in the booth and as a newspaper columnist, he wasn't a hit at the Hall of Fame with the baseball writers.

His first year of eligibility was 1968 and he received only six votes of the 283 cast. He needed 75 percent of the votes to be admitted to the Hall of Fame, but only had 2.1 percent. For the next eight years, he received less than 100 votes in each ballot. His highest percentage was 21.9 percent in 1976.

Beginning in 1977 Richie began gaining additional support from the writers. His top vote total was 158 in 1978, a percentage of 41.7 percent. In his final year of eligibility, 1982, Richie received 126 of 415 votes for a percentage of 30.4 percent.

Richie did have some staunch supporters, such as Pulitzer Prize winner Red Smith. He wrote in the *New York Times*, "I voted for Richie Ashburn because he represented 15 seasons of first-class baseball and ungrudging effort."

If Richie was to enter the Hall of Fame, baseball's Veterans' Committee would have to approve his admittance. Veterans' Committee is the popular name for the committee that has the official designation of National Baseball Hall of Fame Committee on Baseball Veterans.

Each year the committee is allowed to approve a maximum of two players for the Hall of Fame. Richie fared better within the Veterans' Committee and one year he came within two votes. Two of his supporters, Stan Musial and Roy Campanella, were reported to be too ill to cast votes that year.

A Hall of Fame official said the rules governing the election of players to Cooperstown are constantly being changed and refined. The personalities of those involved in the selection process have a lot to do with the rule changes, according to baseball insiders.

A vote in 1984 by the Veterans' Committee appears to have had a disastrous effect on Richie. The committee selected Pee Wee Reese and Rick Ferrell, a catcher who played for 18 seasons with the St. Louis Browns, Boston Red Sox and Washington Senators during his career. Reese wasn't the problem, it was Ferrell.

When Ferrell retired, he had the record for most games played by a catcher, a record that has since been broken. He remained in professional baseball for many years as a coach, scout and team executive after his playing days concluded. Ferrell was an All Star eight times in his career and compiled a

.281 batting average. He was known as the designated catcher when knuckleball pitchers were on the mound. For the most part, he played on mediocre teams.

Ferrell had a good career but the members of the baseball writers' association never felt him to be worthy of inclusion in the Hall of Fame. He never received more than three votes during his eligibility. Ferrell did have his supporters and one writer wrote that he didn't know why Ferrell was kept from the Hall of Fame for so long.

After Ferrell's selection, a new rule was placed on the Veterans' Committee. In 1991, the 60 percent rule was passed. The Veterans' Committee couldn't consider for inclusion in the Hall of Fame any player who began his career after 1945 unless the player had been named on at least 60 percent of the ballots in one election conducted by the baseball writers' association. The ruling made it impossible for many stars, including Yankees Phil Rizzuto and Roger Maris, to be included in the Hall of Fame.

Richie was also banned because the highest percentage he received was 41.7 percent.

Richie became resigned to not being a member of the Hall of Fame. He joked about not wanting to be a member of a club that would have him. He wrote in the *Philadelphia Daily News* in 1983, "Now that the baseball Hall of Fame is inducting broadcasters and writers into their hallowed halls, I stand an excellent chance of being the only man rejected by the Hall of Fame in three different categories."

* * *

The *New York Times* ran an Associated Press story on February 10, 1991, concerning the Veterans' Committee rule change. The story stated, "Anyone who thought that Pete Rose was the only former major leaguer barred from the Hall of Fame on Monday didn't read the fine print of the measure adopted by the hall's directors on a 12-0 vote.

"In addition to barring players on the major league ineligible list, which effectively bans Rose from the hall unless he is restored to the eligible list before 2006, the measure contained a rules change that permanently bars three other outstanding former players. They are Richie Ashburn, the former Philadelphia Phillies center fielder who had a .308 career batting average, and two deceased players, Roger Maris, who set the season home-run record with 61 for the Yankees in 1961, and Harvey Kuenn, an infielder and outfielder who played most of his career with the Detroit Tigers and the San Francisco Giants and had a .303 career average.

"The new rule says that no player who began his career after 1945 and who hasn't received at least 60 percent of the votes cast by members of the Baseball Writers Association of America during any one of his 15 years of initial eligibility can ever be considered for election by the hall's Veterans' Committee.

"It replaced a rule that set the minimum at 100 votes, a number whose percentage of the total has generally declined over the years as the number of voting writers increased. The 100-vote minimum was 22.6 percent of the 443 votes cast in the last election.

"The only former major leaguers affected by the change are Ashburn, who never received more than 42 percent of the vote during his 15 years of eligibility; Maris, who had a high of 43 percent, and Kuenn, who had a high of 39 percent.

"That strikes Ashburn as both surprising and unfair, as he indicated on Thursday in a column he writes for the Philadelphia Daily News. He suggested that Maris and Kuenn would agree.

"'I suspect they would think it strange, as I do, that a special rule would be passed affecting only three players,' Ashburn wrote. 'We should have been given the same consideration every other player has received.'"

* * *

The non-selection to the Hall of Fame paled in comparison to a personal tragedy that marred Richie's world in 1987. While in spring training, Richie received a call that his daughter, Jan, was killed in a single-car accident. The loss of Jan was devastating to Richie, and many said he never recovered from her death. Fans sent thousands of sympathy cards and letters to Richie as word of his daughter's death spread throughout Philadelphia.

Richie wrote a column about the death of his daughter. The headline was: "Smile with Me for Jan." He wrote, "I was in Florida with my two sons, Richard and John, and Richard's wife, Lisa, when I received a call from Lankenau Hospital. The saddest day of my life was sadder when I had to break the news to Jan's mother, Herbie and her older sister, Jean Meredith and two younger sisters." The article noted that Jan Ashburn was born on April 17, 1954, and died on April 1, 1987.

Chris Wheeler, one of Richie's broadcasting partners, said, "Jan was really important to him. He was very close with Jan. She had his laugh. We all said Jan was the girl Richey. She had his sense of humor. They were very close."

Jim Donahue the Fan

WHILE RICHIE ASHBURN was running bases and roaming the outfield with the best of Major League Baseball stars—Willie Mays, Duke Snider and Mickey Mantle—young baseball fan Jim Donahue was growing up not far from the Phillies playing fields of Connie Mack Stadium and later Veterans Stadium in Philadelphia.

Jim utilized lessons learned from his father while sitting in the bleachers at Connie Mack Stadium. He played organized baseball through his high school years. Jim, as with thousands of other young baseball players, realized the love of the game wasn't enough to earn a big league career.

As his school years drew to a close, Jim found another passion. "It was about then I discovered the guitar, and realized I could hit a 'C' chord a lot easier than a curve ball. If you were a music fan in the sixties, you were either a Beatles or Stones fan, and I was a Beatles fan."

Jim pursued his dream of becoming the next Paul McCartney. As a young man he played with friends in neighborhood bands. He practiced for hours with his band mates and spent evenings performing in local bars and clubs. During one of the engagements, Jim met his future wife Joan, a neighborhood girl.

"She had a school uniform on. I was 19 when I met Joan and she was 16. I remember her sweet 16 birthday party. We were married on September 9, 1972. Since our wedding anniversary is nine, nine, the joke is that she should have said nein, nein, or no-no. Joan has put up with all of my craziness over the years."

Jim never became the next Paul McCartney, but he did get a chance to meet his music idol in later life.

The meeting began when his older daughter, Heather, approached him with a business proposition. Heather was an actress in New York City and had recently graduated from college. "She wanted to know if we wanted to invest $5,000 in a movie she was doing with her friends. They had formed Haxan Films. This was a movie without a script and was just a bunch of college kids. I told my wife we could invest in this movie or pay off college bills. We decided to pay the college tuition."

Heather auditioned for a part and won one of the staring roles in *The Blair Witch Project*, one of the highest return-on-investment movies in Hollywood history. The movie cost thousands to make and generated multi-million dollars in income. Jim missed his opportunity to share in the profits.

"The movie caused quite a stir," Jim recalled. "Because of all of the interest, Heather was asked to be a presenter at an *MTV* awards show. She asked my younger daughter Caitlin and me to join her for the show in New York City. Heather told me the last presenter would be someone I would like to meet. I couldn't imagine any of the performers being on my list of favorite stars to meet. They were listed as the Backstreet Boys and INSYNC.

"I was wrong. The last presenter was Paul McCartney. As a fan of the Beatles, that's like finding the Holy Grail. My encounter with Sir Paul was brief, just like my first meeting with Whitey, but it was a memory of a lifetime."

While music and baseball occupied Jim during his early adult years, life's realities intervened. Jim needed an income-producing job. After completing high school in Philadelphia in the late 1960's, Jim entered the workforce and found his first job at Curtis Publishing Company in Philadelphia as an apprentice in the print department. Curtis, a major City of Brotherly Love company for years, went out of business and Jim found another printing employer in the city.

His second printing job lasted 34 years until the business was purchased by a foreign company. The company did financial printing for many major companies, including Merrill Lynch and Drexel Burnham. FCC filings, newsletters and other financial forms filled Jim's working days.

His steady work allowed Jim to provide a good home, education and recreational opportunities for his family, including daughters Heather and Caitlin, and son Ryan. He even found time to be a coach of his children's sports teams.

* * *

Jim never lost contact with Richie Ashburn even though 34 years elapsed from the time he received his autograph in 1957 until his next personal meeting in 1991.

"I was in touch with him just like everyone else in the Delaware Valley," Jim said. "I listened to Whitey on the radio. When we went to the shore we took the radio to listen to him and the Phillies. It didn't matter where we were. It didn't matter if we were on a family picnic or a Sunday drive, we had Richie along with us. That was my connection."

Like his father, Ryan Donahue developed an avid interest in baseball and especially baseball memorabilia collecting. "I went to a sports memorabilia show in 1989 and Ryan went with me," Jim said. "We looked at a lot of the sports material, especially the baseball cards. I recognized a lot of them as the ones I had as a kid. Later I went to my Mom's house and dug out all of the old cards and also the autograph books. This was the time of the big boom in baseball cards. Some of them were selling for a lot of money.

"Ryan became very interested in the sports cards. My son is a big baseball fan. We began spending weekends going to shows. There were lots of shows in those days. Every mall seemed to have a show and many hotels hosted them. Also, major league players and retired players were attending and signing autographs. I know them as the 'praise and pay' sessions. You stood in line, paid a fee, praised the player and received his autograph. I wasn't a big purchaser of the autographs but Ryan was interested and always wanted to collect signatures."

Delaware Valley shows were listed in a weekly column in the *Philadelphia Daily News*. On a summer's day in August 1991, Jim and Ryan decided to travel to the Woodbine Inn in Pennsauken, New Jersey, for such an event.

One of the star attractions of the show at the Woodbine Inn was Jim's boyhood baseball idol Richie "Whitey" Ashburn.

Why the Hall Not

THE WOODBINE INN had a room full of dealers. They were selling collectable memorabilia from baseball and other sports. They even offered some photographs and other signed items of major league players.

Jim Donahue's goal that day in August was to obtain a signed baseball to add to his collection. He wasn't looking to start a crusade. He just wanted a baseball with the signature of his favorite player, Richie "Whitey" Ashburn.

Jim purchased a ticket from the show's promoter and went to the back of the line to patiently wait his turn to see Richie. As Jim stood in the long line, he began to engage in conversation with other baseball fans. A number of Richie's fans were at the event that day and their discussions turned to the subject of the Hall of Fame. Earlier in the year the eligibility rule was changed and Richie seemed barred forever from attaining a spot in Cooperstown.

"Many of the fans in line were saying it was a shame that Richie wouldn't be in the Hall of Fame. We all agreed it was an unfair situation and Richie had earned a spot in Cooperstown," Jim said. "Many at the show were knowledgeable baseball fans. They knew Richie's lifetime statistics. We exchanged stories of Richie's playing days."

The excitement of Richie's fans and the talk of the injustice surrounding the Hall of Fame situation moved Jim to make a split-second decision that would dominate his life for the next four years.

"As the line moved forward, the Hall of Fame talk continued," Jim said. "When it came my turn, I handed the baseball to Richie and asked for his signature. I also told him it seemed unfair that he would never again be eligible for inclusion in the Hall of Fame. I then asked him how he would feel if his fans started a petition drive to overturn the rule."

Richie signed the ball, stopped and gave Jim a quizzical look.

"Richie told me I looked like a perfectly reasonable and intelligent guy," Jim recalled. "He then asked me why I would waste my time on such a project."

Jim saw an opening as Richie didn't flat out say no to the idea of a fan-based petition drive.

"I pressed Richie and asked if he would object to the project," Jim said. "He said he wouldn't object." Jim took the answer to mean he had Richie's permission to mount a fan-based campaign.

Jim's second meeting with Richie lasted about as long as the time he received his first autograph from Richie, a few minutes. They both were significant events in the life of Jim Donahue.

Driving back to his Delaware County home from the Woodbine Inn show with his son, Jim began thinking about the project he had just proposed to Richie. "I thought about how the petition drive could take place and who would support it. I knew from the show that many people agreed with me that Richie deserved a spot in Cooperstown," Jim said.

The more Jim thought about the project, the more he became engaged and committed to seeing the campaign succeed. "I knew we needed something catchy to call the petition drive so it would get the attention of the public. The message had to be simple. I thought it was obvious that the campaign should be called "Why the Hall Not?" The message would fit on bumper stickers. It was perfect."

Jim had an idea, a message and a crusade. His next step was to begin to enlist supporters for Why the Hall Not?

One of the first persons Jim thought could help the project was Ted Taylor. Taylor wrote a sports memorabilia column for *Sports Collector Digest*. Taylor also wrote a column in the *Philadelphia Daily News*.

"Collecting of sports memorabilia was a big business at the time," Jim said. "Some collectors looked at their prized possessions as a form of investing. The *Sports Collector Digest* was printed in Wisconsin. Ted had written about Richie and he was also a fan of the old Philadelphia A's team. I had some bumper stickers printed with the slogan and sent them to him. I decided to sell the bumper stickers and give all of the proceeds to the ALS charity in Richie's name. It would be a contribution from Richie's fans and it would be a way to publicize the petition drive."

In late September 1991, Jim wrote a letter to Taylor and sent him the information on the campaign. A month later, Taylor wrote a column in *Sports Collector Digest* concerning the campaign and included information on how to get in touch with Jim. The article ran a full page. "I don't know the circulation of the publication at the time but it was major. The column created great national interest and I started to get requests from across the county. People wanted bumper stickers and petitions that they could circulate," Jim said.

Taylor also followed up his article in *Sports Collector Digest* with another one in the *Philadelphia Daily News*.

"Sports collecting has been my hobby my whole life," Taylor said. "I began collecting when I was seven years old. I actually began collecting not with sports but Roy Rogers and his Sons of the Pioneers musical group. I was sitting in a restaurant in Bath, New York, when I saw them and introduced myself. Roy wasn't there but they were doing an appearance at a local movie theater. I got their autographs. They were the first signatures I collected.

"I collect baseball cards and have always enjoyed baseball. I was nine years old when The Whiz Kids won the pennant. The irony is I was an A's fan. My Dad was an A's fan. My favorite on the Phillies was Del Ennis and not Richie Ashburn. Ennis hit home runs. Over the years I came to appreciate Richie. My ultimate favorite on the Phillies was Robin Roberts."

Taylor began a sports card and memorabilia show in Willow Grove, Pennsylvania, that drew 15,000 visitors during a weekend. He was an athletic director with Spring Garden College. Taylor said he first met Donahue during one of his memorabilia shows.

"He (Donahue) contacted me about the Why the Hall Not? campaign and I thought it was a good idea. I ran articles in both columns and I hope it helped. It never hurts to have a story in a daily newspaper with a large circulation. Jim believed in what he was doing. He was sincere and a nice guy. He was not doing anything other than trying to help Richie. I had no problems promoting what Jim was doing and helping him gain coverage."

Taylor also liked Ashburn. "Richie called my house one day and my wife answered. She said it was Richie Ashburn on the phone and 'he sounds just like himself.' I said, 'That's who he is.' It was fun to be part of the campaign," Taylor said. "I ran a show in Ocean City, New Jersey, and Richie was scheduled to be there for two hours. There was still a line for his autograph when his time ended but he stayed there another 45 minutes and never asked for another nickel."

Taylor has another story about Richie that includes Taylor's cousin, Jeff Stevens. Stevens has a business in Cooperstown, New York, where he merchandizes Hall of Fame articles. Stevens visited Richie's home one day to collect Richie's autograph on items for his business. "Ashburn greeted Jeff and signed the material and asked Jeff he was hungry," Taylor recalled. "Richie made him a sandwich and the two of them talked for an hour or two."

When Jim Donahue approached Taylor about the campaign, Taylor admits he didn't think the drive would succeed. "I often advocated for guys who should have been in the Hall of Fame but were not. I thought Richie was one of them and I wrote about him. Statistically, he belonged there. He was also a long-time fixture as a broadcaster. "

Jim said, "When the campaign began, I was looking for 10,000 signatures. I wanted to set a goal with a significant number. I thought having a petition with 10,000 signatures would prove to the Hall of Fame that baseball fans believed Richie belonged in Cooperstown."

Toward the end of the year, Jim received a card from Richie. Richie wrote to Jim that his mother saw articles on the Why the Hall Not? campaign and got a laugh out of the effort on his behalf. Richie's mother also wanted some of the bumper stickers and Jim mailed them to her. The note concluded with Richie wishing Jim luck. Richie also stated that he believed Jim was "beating a dead horse."

Richie informed Jim that he didn't think it was right for him to become personally involved in the campaign and promote himself. Jean Ashburn, Richie's daughter, said the same belief was held by Richie's family. The family appreciated Jim's efforts, she said.

* * *

Not all of the publicity Jim received was favorable. Jim learned some hard lessons about dealing with reporters and the media.

A freelance reporter approached Jim about doing an article for *Sports Illustrated*. Having a story in the national magazine would greatly enhance the visibility of the project and Jim spent three hours being interviewed by the reporter. Jim detailed the campaign strategy and stated why he believed Richie should be in the Hall of Fame.

The article never appeared in *Sports Illustrated* but *Philadelphia Magazine* did publish an item from the reporter.

"The last thing I needed and Richie needed was this type of publicity," Jim said. "After talking to me for three hours, he misquoted me. He wanted me to come off as an inarticulate fan. The only quote attributed to me was, 'I ain't trying to stop wars or nothing.' I didn't say anything like that. I think the writer was trying to denigrate Philadelphia sports fans. The author was trying to make us look like ignorant buffoons. We're not. I wrote a letter of complaint to *Philadelphia Magazine* and the magazine published my letter."

Soon after the *Philadelphia Magazine* article was published, Jim attended another memorabilia show where Richie was signing autographs. This signing took place at the Mitchell and Ness sports nostalgia store in center city Philadelphia. Mitchell and Ness was established in 1904 and continues to sell authentic sports apparel.

"I just showed up for the show," Jim said. "By this time Richie knew me by sight. He laughed and announced to the people in line that I was a guy who had lots of time to waste. I informed him of my plan for the campaign and gave him some bumper stickers. He added that it was my time to waste.

Richie had also read the offending *Philadelphia Magazine* article and told Jim not to be too depressed or concerned about the item. "He told me I would have to put up with those types of articles and I should be prepared to deal with more of them," Jim said. "He said the media worked with sound bites. It was a good education for me. The experience taught me how to talk to the media. Richie also said the campaign was going to be a good, hard climb to succeed and it wouldn't be done easily."

Encouraged by Richie's comments, Jim began setting goals for the campaign. He wanted to have enough signatures to influence the Hall of Fame rules committee by early 1994. Jim was sure that two stars of the Philadelphia Phillies, Mike Schmidt and Steve Carlton, would be enshrined in Cooperstown in the coming years and he wanted Richie to join one of the two during the Hall of Fame induction ceremony.

* * *

Jim's campaign had received national exposure and attracted the attention of many in the baseball world, including the management of the Philadelphia Phillies. In early 1992, Jim received a call from the Phillies. He was invited to a meeting at Veterans Stadium to discuss the petition campaign.

"I never wrote a letter directly to the Phillies. I didn't know anyone there. I didn't know anyone at the Hall of Fame. I wanted the effort on behalf of Richie to be a grassroots one by his fans. I didn't ask for any help," Jim said.

Jim had no idea who would be in the meeting with the Phillies' brass. "The meeting included Larry Shenk, the resident team historian; President Bill Giles; and Curt Funk, now director of marketing. He was designated to be my babysitter. They wanted to make sure I didn't do anything inappropriate. Dave Raymond, who was the original Phillies Phanatic mascot, was at the meeting. Dave was a good friend of Richie's and he told me he wanted to see Richie become a member of the Hall of Fame."

Jim knew he was an outsider, not a member of the Phillies' family. "Bill Giles said he heard about my campaign and asked about my marketing background. The Phillies' organization takes pride in the team's marketing campaigns. I told them I was doing this because of my love of the game. I didn't have any marketing experience. I was coming from the perspective of Joe-average fan. I told them that if I felt Richie should be in the Hall of Fame, I knew other fans felt exactly the same way I did."

Jim told the Phillies that he didn't want them to feel obligated to get involved in his campaign and he didn't want anything specific from the club. "I told them I wanted to keep the campaign as simple a possible. I didn't want a glossy, glitzy campaign. I wanted it to be a fans' grassroots campaign. I didn't have the resources for a Madison Avenue campaign. I thought as signatures began to trickle in, they would build and it would turn from one voice into a chorus. I told them I was committed to seeing the campaign through to its conclusion. I also told them of my goal of having Richie enter the Hall with either Mike Schmidt or Steve Carlton."

Schmidt and Carlton were two of the Phillies all-time superstars. Schmidt, a slick-fielding third baseman, was a clutch power-hitter for the Phillies. Schmidt played for the Phillies from 1972 until 1989. Carlton, known as "Lefty," at times was almost unhittable. He won four Cy Young awards. He started 499 games, more games than any other Phillies' pitcher. He struck out 3,031 batters, a Phillies' record. Lefty's 241 career wins as a Phillies' player is tops in franchise history.

Shenk warned Jim that fans can't vote Richie into the Hall of Fame. Jim commented, "I told him that I realized that was the case but if enough fans rallied to show that the rule change was unjust, it would be changed. I think Bill Giles realized I was serious. I told them I was going to work on the project in my spare time and I was willing to give up time with my family. I said my wife understood the time commitment.

"I thought the Phillies might profit from the campaign. The team wasn't selling out during those seasons," Jim said.

When the meeting concluded, Jim showed them his Why the Hall Not? bumper stickers. "The Phillies management wasn't sure about the slogan and they indicated the slogan might be a stumbling block. They were afraid of offending some of their fans." Jim only asked to be allowed to solicit signatures for his petition at Veterans Stadium. If not at the stadium, he asked for permission to collect signatures at the subway stop at Broad and Pattison avenues, the subway stop near Veterans Stadium.

"After the meeting ended, we shook hands and I went home, By the time I reached home there was a voice message on my answering machine. I was told I would be allowed to set up a table at all Sunday games, opening day and week-day business persons' games. The only objection they had concerned the campaign's slogan. Richie's mother loved the slogan and she was in her 80s. I didn't see why fans would object. They offered to make up a silk banner with another slogan. I submitted a ridiculous slogan, one that barely fit on a 6-foot by 3-foot banner. The message was Willie (Mays), Mickey (Mantle), Richie (Ashburn) and the Duke (Snider) all belong in the Hall of Fame in Cooperstown, New York. The wording would never have fit on a bumper sticker. The banner was made but never used."

* * *

The Phillies' management was concerned about Jim and his campaign. "I was leery at the beginning," Shenk said. "We didn't want to do anything that would rub Cooperstown the wrong way. Helping Richie gain a place in the Hall of Fame was a sensitive issue. We all hoped Richie would enter the Hall of Fame but we weren't sure he would. Bill Giles and writer Allen Lewis were working behind the scenes to help Richie. Attaining a place in the Hall of Fame isn't the same (public popularity contest) as winning a Heisman Trophy."

Lewis was a long-time *Philadelphia Inquirer* sports reporter and a member of the Hall of Fame's Veterans' Committee from 1979 until 2000. He won the J. G. Taylor Spink Award and is included in the writers' wing of the Hall of Fame.

The J. G. Taylor Spink Award was first given in 1962 in an effort to recognize the baseball writer for his or her meritorious contributions to the field of baseball writing. The recipients are selected by the Baseball Writers Association of America annually and voted on during baseball's winter meetings. The winner is announced during the annual induction ceremonies at the National Baseball Hall of Fame and presented with a certificate recognized on the "Scribes & Mikemen" exhibit in the Hall of Fame.

"I remember Larry (Shenk) telling me about the Why the Hall Not? campaign," Chris Wheeler said. Wheeler began working for the Phillies in the public relations department and later broadcasted games with Richie and Harry Kalas. "Larry told me about a guy that was calling him and sending him stuff. Larry and the Phillies thought the campaign was a great idea."

Wheeler believes Lewis was the key to getting Richie selected to the Hall of Fame. "Allen Lewis was Richie's main proponent. In those days if you had a sponsor on the committee, such as Allen, you could get elected. Allen was a huge supporter of Richie."

* * *

While Allen Lewis, Bill Giles and others in the Phillies' organization quietly worked behind the scenes for Richie, Jim's campaign was more public and fan-based, according to Shenk.

9

The Campaign

THE PHILLIES' HIERARCHY gave Jim Donahue a reason to believe the Why the Hall Not? campaign had a chance of succeeding. The Phillies were allowing him access to the team's fan base at Veterans Stadium.

"I think the Phillies wanted to find out something about me and my motive for running this campaign. All I ever wanted, and other fans had the same motive, was to have Richie Ashburn in the Hall of Fame. We believed he deserved to be in the Hall on merit. He was a Hall of Famer."

Jim's challenge was to spread the word about the campaign to the Philadelphia sports world and beyond. After the meeting with the Phillies, he received another big boost from a call-in radio sports station covering the Delaware Valley.

Jim was a fan of the morning radio show of WIP radio. He believed one of the hosts, Angelo Cataldi, would be interested in the Ashburn campaign. "Angelo likes the underdog type of story," Donahue said. Donahue sent Cataldi T-shirts, bumper stickers and Ashburn petitions. WIP had a big audience of sports fans and the station would be a key component in accumulating thousands of signatures.

While Jim was working the third shift at the printing plant where he was employed, a co-worker came in to start his shift and said he had just heard the WIP hosts talking about the Why the Hall Not? campaign. "As soon as I had a chance, I called the show and talked to one of the producers. They put me on the air and I began talking about Richie Ashburn and the Hall of Fame. At the time, every week the hosts broadcast a show at the Franklin Plaza Hotel at 17th and Race streets in Philadelphia. I told the hosts I would appear that Friday at the hotel and talk about the campaign.

"I had a chance to talk with Angelo off the air and he was very supportive of the efforts to get Richie into the Hall of Fame. He was gracious and nice to me. Angelo offered to help in any way he could. They wanted to figure out a way to make my appearance more interesting, instead of just a talk with a guy soliciting signatures. The show has always been fun and a little outrageous at times. We discussed some ideas and it was decided I would issue a challenge to another one of the hosts, Al Morganti, about Richie's being elected to the Hall of Fame. Even though Al liked Richie and thought he should be in Cooperstown, he was going to play devil's advocate and say Richie shouldn't be elected. The hosts did a lot of good cop and bad cop routines on the show. I was the good cop and Al would be the bad cop.

"Al is a Red Sox fan. When I was on the show I bet Al that Richie would make the Hall of Fame. I said if he failed to do so, I would pay $1 for every hit Richie had in the major leagues to Al's favorite charity. Richie had 2,574 hits in his career. I mentioned during the show that I hoped my wife wasn't listening as she would not like my betting $2,574 on the outcome of the campaign.

"Of course we had to come up with something for Al to bet when Richie went into the Hall of Fame. You have to remember this show is based on humor and there was no way it was intended for Al to pay off his bet if he lost. We agreed Al had to meet me at home plate at Doubleday Field in Cooperstown on the day Richie was inducted into the Hall of Fame and kiss my butt. When the announcement was made that Richie had been elected, I called the station and sent

several ChapSticks® and other trinkets to Al to help him get
ready to pay off the bet.

"The morning show crew at WIP was fabulous all during
the campaign. They would call and ask how the campaign was
doing. Angelo is such a nice guy. He said, 'Let's get Whitey
into the Hall of Fame.' Angelo and Ted Taylor were the two
of my key supporters in getting out the word about the campaign. They helped to keep the campaign alive."

* * *

The Phillies opened the 1992 season on April 7, 1992, at
Veterans Stadium against the Chicago Cubs. Manager Jim
Fregosi selected Terry Mulholland as the opening day pitcher
for the Phillies. Cubs' ace Greg Maddux opposed Mulholland
as 60,431 fans jammed the stadium.

One of the fans was Jim Donahue, except he didn't get to
see much of the contest. Donahue was at the game to collect
signatures for the Why the Hall Not? campaign. The Phillies
allowed Jim to set up his table on the lower level concourse in
back of home plate near the Hall of Fame wall. Mulholland
and the Phillies lost 4-3 to Maddux and the Cubs.

Jim and a friend, Tony Baselice, were the ones manning the
table on opening day. Prior to the game, Jim went to an office
supply store and purchased clipboards and other items. He
had petitions copied at his work and he brought along his own
folding table and chairs. "I wanted to make the table colorful
to draw fans to the table," Jim said. "I had Richie golf hats,
photographs and posters of Richie and other items."

On opening day, Jim drove to the stadium, unloaded his
petitions, T-shirts, bumper stickers and Ashburn memorabilia.
He parked his car and then entered Veterans Stadium to set
up his station. Before Jim unloaded his boxes of petitions and
was ready to accept signatures, he had his first customer.

"I was turned away from the table getting items from a box," Jim recalled. "A guy asked, 'Is this where I sign up to get Richie in the Hall of Fame?' The familiar voice was Ed Rendell, the then Mayor of Philadelphia. He later became Governor of Pennsylvania. He was a fan of Richie Ashburn and a big sports fan of all of the Philadelphia teams. We made some small talk and then I gave him one of my Why the Hall Not? T-shirts."

Rendell was the first, but certainly not the last of Philadelphia celebrities to sign the Ashburn petition. Ashburn's broadcasting partner Harry Kalas signed along with Phillies' owner Bill Giles. Mike Schmidt and Lenny Dykstra of the Phillies were among those to sign. Professional basketball player Charles Barkley lent his support. Paul Richardson, who played the organ at the Phillies, joined the growing number of signers.

"Also stopping by the table were Angelo Cataldi and Tony Bruno of the WIP morning radio show. Tony has since moved to the ESPN affiliate in Philadelphia. They hung around and helped for a time. It was a cool thing and they helped break the ice with some of the fans," Jim said. "They stirred up the crowd. Many sports fans knew their voices, if not their faces. When they heard Angelo and Tony at the table, they came over to see what was taking place. It was a big day for me and the campaign. Many of the fans asked for petitions so they could collect signatures. Some of the petitions we later received were photocopies of the originals. Each one had 33 lines for signatures. Generation after generation of copies were made from those original petitions."

* * *

Every Sunday that the Phillies played home games, Jim set up with wooden folding table. He pulled into the entrance near Veterans Stadium and unloaded his boxes and parked his car.

At the end of each game he would reverse the process, pack his boxes, take them to the entrance and then retrieve his car. Later in the season, he did manage to secure a parking spot a little closer to the entrance.

He conducted his crusade with little fanfare. There were no announcements made by the Phillies on the public address system during the games. He manned his table and collected his signatures. Some of the days were extremely long. He remembered one Sunday late in the 1992 season when the Phillies were playing a doubleheader against the San Diego Padres. Two games were needed because a contest had been rained out earlier in the year.

"That day I arrived about 9:00 a.m. and set up my table and I stayed for both games. I was on the Hall of Fame concourse and I didn't see a play of either game. I could hear the roar of the crowd so I knew when something good or bad was taking place for the Phillies. I was there the full twelve hours and didn't get home until probably about 10:00 p.m."

Jim's streak of not missing a Sunday at the ballpark was threatened by his 20th wedding anniversary. "I had promised my wife that we would do something special for the occasion. We decided to take a cruise to nowhere. I booked a three-day cruise that left on Friday afternoon. We were to dock on Sunday morning. Joan jokes that after 20 years of marriage we went on a cruise to nowhere and it took us two and a half days to get there.

"As we were docking, she noticed I was looking at my watch. I hadn't mentioned that the Phillies were playing that day. She said, 'It's a home game and you want to go.' I told her it was our anniversary and I wasn't planning to go. My friend, Tony Baselice, was going to man the table. He had helped several times during the season. Joan said, 'If you want to go, go.'"

Jim drove his wife home and then raced to the stadium where he arrived before the first pitch. "This story is a credit to my wife. She was so supportive during the campaign. She supported me and my hare-brained idea. When I brought up the idea, she asked me if I thought the campaign would be successful. I told her I thought it would. I really, really always believed that one day Richie Ashburn would be in the Hall of Fame."

* * *

While Jim was making headway on his goal of having Ashburn in Cooperstown, the Phillies were having a subpar year on the field. The team finished with a 70-92 record, good for sixth place in the National League East. The team did draw a large number of fans as paid attendance was 1,927,448 for the year.

"It was a long season. The team wasn't great but the nucleus was there for the next year. Darren Daulton, John Kruk, Denny Dykstra, Curt Schilling and Dave Hollins were all playing for the Phillies. The team had a lot of tough breaks early in the season and the year didn't play out as everyone expected," Jim said.

As the 1992 season progressed, Jim's relationship with Ashburn grew stronger. "We developed a better rapport, especially after the All-Star game," Donahue said. "Richie was reluctant at first to get involved because he believed it was self-serving and I understood. The first note he wrote me said he appreciated the effort but he couldn't get involved. After we met at Mitchell & Ness, I received a personal note. He thanked me for my efforts but he still believed I was flogging a dead horse. He used that dead horse phrase a lot with Harry Kalas."

* * *

As the Phillies faltered on the field, the campaign was taking hold across the United States and internationally. One petition arrived from Japan. A Phillies' fan who was a member of the Merchant Marines had read about the Why the Hall Not? campaign. The fan gathered signatures from his shipmates and forwarded the petition to Jim.

"I received petitions from just about every state in the nation. I think I didn't get one from Wyoming. I was amazed," Jim said. "Of course, Richie's home state of Nebraska embraced the campaign. Richie's niece helped a lot. Those in Tilden, Richie's home town, were excited that someone from their area might get into the Hall of Fame."

Ashburn's mother, Toots, also was involved in the campaign. "I had a number of telephone conversations with her," Jim said. "She was the sweetest woman. She was down to earth. She was a wonderful lady and had the same personality as her son. She told me that the local pharmacist in Tilden had a display honoring Richie in his store. The man took part in getting the community involved in the campaign. Everyone there was excited. Richey brought pride to Tilden. It was a big deal."

Jim thought 10,000 signatures after the first year would constitute a successful season. When the names were tallied, he had amassed about 50,000. "It was a significant amount, enough I believed to get noticed in Cooperstown," Jim said.

The opportunities for positive publicity continued for the Why the Hall Not? campaign. The *Philadelphia Inquirer* wrote a story on the petition drive and Jim had an opportunity to appear on a national half-hour radio show called *Sports Byline USA* originating in San Francisco. The opportunity came from the campaign's friend, Ted Taylor, who wrote about Ashburn and the Hall of Fame for the *Philadelphia Daily News* and *Sports Collector Digest*.

"I did many different things, including the *Sports Byline USA* radio show," Taylor said. "It was a syndicated show from 11:00 p.m. until midnight every Friday night. I did the show from here in the Delaware Valley. The show had a huge audience."

"Ted did some work for Fleer, the baseball card company," Jim Donahue said. "On Friday nights he appeared on *Sports Byline USA* for a sports collector segment. One night he had me on the show as a guest. I fielded questions why Richie should be in the Hall of Fame. I was ready; I had put together a booklet with Richie's statistics. I had the number of hits he had, stolen bases and information on his batting crowns. I never argued with people. I also never compared Richie to those already in the Hall of Fame with inferior statistics. I never criticized anyone connected with the Hall of Fame. I was careful what I said. I respected Richie Ashburn and I wanted the campaign handled with dignity.

"The show had a nationwide audience. That was excellent since I had no money for promotion. The beauty of this campaign was that it was about as basic as it could be. I never once asked for a contribution. After each exposure in the press, I received additional signatures and also requests for bumper stickers. The shows also gave me an additional burst of energy.

"Running a national campaign and working a regular job created a weird situation for me. I'd come home from work and have letters from people all across the country. They had read articles in various publications and they wanted to help. They would copy the original petitions and have them signed. It was exciting to me having all those people willing to get behind the Why the Hall Not? campaign. Richie was a very public figure as the Phillies' broadcaster. That didn't hurt. For those who didn't remember him as a player, he was known as a broadcaster and writer.

"Some of the petitions had ten signatures and some of the petitions had all 33 slots filled. I received many letters from fans saying how Richie affected them, many that mirrored my own story. They remembered Richie signing autographs for them when they were young. I realized there was nothing unique about me. There were lots of people that Richie touched. I was no different than thousands of other fans who wanted to help Richie get into the Hall of Fame.

"I knew that if the campaign failed, it wouldn't be the worst thing that could happen to me. The worst thing would not be trying."

* * *

The 1993 baseball season was a lot different for the Philadelphia Phillies as the team went from sixth place to winning the National League East pennant with a record of 97-65, a 27 game improvement over the previous year. The team also increased its attendance to 3,137,674, giving Donahue the chance to secure a multitude of additional signatures for his petition drive.

In the National League Championship Series, the Phillies faced the Atlanta Braves. With Curt Schilling earning the Most Valuable Player honor, the Phillies won the series four games to two.

Phillies reliever Mitch Williams won the first game of the Atlanta series but he would be the losing pitcher in the last game of the World Series as the Toronto Blue Jays were crowned baseball champions. With the Phillies winning 6-5 in the bottom of the ninth inning of game six, Toronto's Joe Carter crushed a Williams' pitch to deep left field for a game winning home run to close out the series four games to two games in favor of the Blue Jays.

While the Phillies had a winning season on the field, Donahue saw the first of his goals accomplished. In July 1993, the rule that Donahue deemed so unjust was overturned. Richie Ashburn was eligible to be considered by the Veterans' Committee of the Hall of Fame. The reason for the rule change isn't clear. One Hall of Fame official said rules are constantly being refined.

Jim's remaining task was to show the Veterans' Committee that the fans supported Richie Ashburn's election to Cooperstown.

As the 1993 baseball season came to a conclusion, the signature campaign continued to remain strong. "We were close to the 100,000 mark at that point," Jim said. "We had been collecting signatures for almost two years. When we began, I thought 10,000 would be a lot of signatures and then it went to 25,000 and then 50,000 and now it was at 100,000. The signatures weren't just generated in the tri-state area. They were coming from all over the place. It was an international effort. I remember petitions coming in from Germany, Holland and servicemen overseas. You have to remember this was before the Internet and You Tube. I always wondered how many signatures we could have gathered if we had had the Internet. This was the world of snail mail. The whole campaign was amazing."

* * *

Not every promotional idea when off as planned. The Lucky the Horse ad placed in Rich Westcott's *Phillies' Report* was one. "Rich's publication reported on all things Phillies. It was very popular and hit my target audience. The fans were so supportive. Rich offered to give me an ad in the publication. I thought I would run one of the original letters that Richie had sent to me. He closed the letter with line: 'Good luck Jim, I hope you aren't flogging a dead horse.'

"At the time I had a friend living on Gradyville Road in Delaware County, outside of Philadelphia. He was raising miniature ponies. I had the clever idea of getting a photograph of one of the horses, Lucky, and place it in the advertisement with the words 'This horse ain't dead yet.'

"The advertisement was placed in the publication and Rich Westcott gave me an advance copy. I was going to take it to the ballpark the next day to show it to Richie. In the meantime my friend who owned Lucky called in a panic. He asked if the publication had been printed. When I told him that it had, he told me that Lucky had just fallen into his pond and drowned. I didn't think that was a good omen for the Why the Hall Not? campaign.

"The next day, an hour before the game, I went to the broadcast booth to show Richie the ad. Harry Kalas was there in the booth. They both liked the ad and laughed at the flogging a dead horse line. I then told them that poor Lucky had died. During the broadcast, Harry made a comment saying he was sorry about Richie's fan, Lucky. Harry didn't explain the story about the horse on the air and I think only the three of us understood the reference. Later, I was given three of Lucky's small horseshoes and I gave one to Richie and another one to Harry.

"Harry was a great supporter of Richie and many times would say during the broadcasts that Richie deserved to be in the Hall of Fame. Many Sundays, Harry would see me before the game and ask about the progress of the campaign. I would give him an updated total of the number of signatures and he would mention Why the Hall Not? during the broadcast. He would say, 'His Whiteness (Richie) deserves to be in the Hall of Fame.' He was a very, very good friend of Richie and he was so proud when Richie finally made it into the Hall of Fame. I can't say enough about Harry. Harry was always great to Richie Ashburn.

"Richie wouldn't comment when Harry made the references. He didn't want to promote himself."

* * *

The 1994 season began with high hopes for the Phillies and the Why the Hall Not? campaign. The team had just competed in the World Series and the nucleus of the squad was intact. Pitchers Curt Schilling and Danny Jackson were the top starters. Jackson would be named to the All-Star team in 1994. Team leaders Lenny Dykstra, Darren Daulton and John Kruk were back for another season.

Jim Donahue was ready for the season. He sent correspondence to the Hall of Fame concerning the election of Richie Ashburn. The Hall of Fame never officially acknowledged the campaign, which had almost 200,000 supporters. Jim understood the reluctance of the Cooperstown officials to correspond with him. "They didn't want to encourage other groups to organize campaigns, especially athletes with issues. Pete Rose was one of those players. He had been banned from baseball for betting on games but he has lots of fans who believe he should be in the Hall of Fame," Jim said.

A large shadow was passing over the 1994 season as opening day approached. The players and management couldn't reach an agreement on a contract and a strike loomed. On August 12, 1994, the players decided to call it a season. Negotiations between both sides continued for almost a month. The management waited until September 14 and then decided to cancel the rest of the season, including the World Series. The season was the eighth time in major league history that a work stoppage had halted play. The strike also resulted in the first time a major sports league lost a postseason because of an unsettled contract.

The owners were worried about the financial stability of the game and decided the only way to survive would be to impose a salary cap. The owners especially were worried about clubs playing in small market cities. Without increased revenue, the owners believed those clubs couldn't survive.

The players, distrustful of the financial reports released by owners, were opposed to a salary cap. The players believed a cap would limit the players' earnings and would allow management to keep an unfair amount of the profits.

The Phillies' hopes for another contending team in 1994 had fizzled by the time of the strike. The team never led the

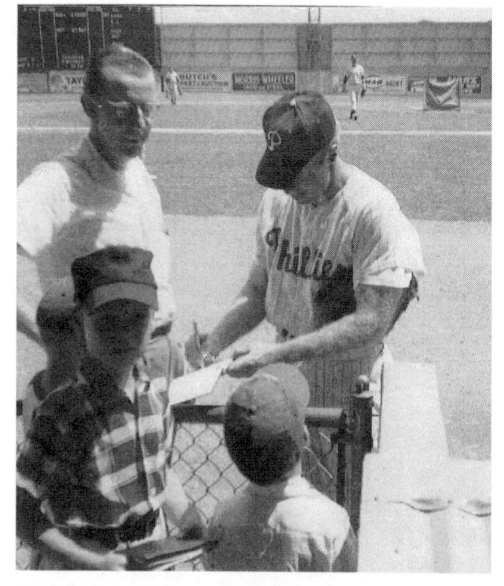

Richie Ashburn and young Jim Donahue in 1957

Jim Donahue and Richie Ashburn at the Philadelphia Mitchell & Ness store in 1991. Ashburn is holding a Why The Hall Not? item

Jim with Ted Taylor during November 1991. As a columnist for the Philadelphia Daily News and Sports Collector's Digest, Ted was instrumental in getting Jim's campaign for Richie launched.

Hall of Fame display of items relating to Phillies' Whiz Kids.

Former Philadelphia Mayor Ed Rendell and wife, Judge Midge Rendell, at Richie's Hall of Fame induction ceremony.

Actor Paul Gleason and Richie at the Hall of Fame induction ceremony.

Phillies' announcers Harry Kalas (standing left center) and Chris "Wheels" Wheeler (to Harry's right) at the 1995 induction ceremony.

Phillies greats Richie Ashburn and Mike Schmidt show off their Hall of Fame plaques. Shown are from left, Donald Marr, Richie Ashburn, Mike Schmidt and Edward Stack, former Chairman of the Hall of Fame

Richie addressing the crowd at his induction in 1995.

Jim at the Hall of Fame induction ceremony.

Richie is pictured with Jim's daughter, Caitlin, in Cooperstown in 1995.

Richie Ashburn's mother, Toots, and sister, Bette, at the activities in Cooperstown.

From left to right: Chuck Hoffman, Genevieve "Toots" Ashburn, Claire Johnson, Kristen (Richie Ashburn's niece) and Jim Donahue at Hall of Fame induction ceremony.

Scoreboard salute during Richie Ashburn Night on Saturday, July 22, 1995, at Veterans Stadium.

Another tribute to Richie at Veterans Stadium that same night.

Bill, a longtime Richie Ashburn fan, joins Jim Donahue alongside a poster of a Richie Ashburn baseball card at Veteran Stadium in 1992.

Richie with Jim and Caitlin Donahue at the 1996 Hall of Fame ceremony. The trio had returned to Cooperstown the following year to see the induction of former Phillie and then–U.S. Senator, Jim Bunning.

Richie Ashburn memorabilia.

INDUCTION CEREMONY
Reserved Seating

July 30, 1995
2:30 p.m
Clark Sports Center Grounds
Gates Open at 1:30 p.m.

In the event of rain, this ticket allows admission to the ceremony
inside the Clark Sports Center
Roundtrip Transportation Provided from Otesaga   **2**

*Hall of Fame induction
ticket for Richie Ashburn's
ceremony at Cooperstown.*

Richie Ashburn....

WHY THE HALL NOT?

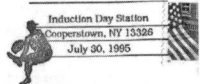

This was the postmarked bumper sticker from the campaign to get Richie in the Hall of Fame.

division and finished with a 54-61 record, 20.5 games behind the Montreal Expos, winner of the Eastern Division of the National League. Dave Hollins and Lenny Dykstra both missed a significant number of games because of injuries. The Phillies were barely ahead of the Florida Marlins, just three games from the bottom of the newly aligned division.

The Phillies did have one of their stars, Steve Carlton, known affectionately as "Lefty," elected to the Hall of Fame by the Baseball Writers Association of American in the first year he was eligible to be elected. Carlton received 95.6 percent of the votes cast. The Veterans' Committee also met and selected two all-time greats, Leo Durocher and Phil Rizzuto.

The strike continued for more than 230 days and play didn't resume until the next season on April 25, 1995. Federal Judge Sonia Sotomayor finally issued a preliminary injunction against the owners on March 31, 1995. The players took the field under the conditions of the previous contract. The strike did great harm to baseball resulting in attendance at games and viewership on television both dropping during the 1995 season.

Judge Sotomayor became a member of the United States Supreme Court in August 2009.

The strike slowed the efforts of Jim Donahue to gather signatures to support Richie's election to the Hall of Fame. The fans were unhappy with the operation of Major League Baseball. "It was a backlash against baseball but not Richie," Donahue said.

There was a positive side to the strike; the break in the playing of games gave Jim a chance to know Richie.

Jim needed to confer with Richie on several aspects of the Why the Hall Not? campaign. Richie suggested they meet for lunch at his home in Ardmore. That one-time invitation for lunch resulted in many more invitations for lunch and evening visits to watch *Jeopardy* on television.

"Richie liked *Jeopardy* and I liked *Jeopardy*," Jim recalled. "We would sit in his living room and we would scream out the answers to see who had the correct one first. We were very competitive. Richie was always very competitive. You could see his makeup when he played baseball, tennis or squash. I remember conversations with Richie, he was very well read. He wrote columns for the *Daily News* and he had a great library in his home.

"After those sessions with Richie, I would drive home and inevitably I'd be at a red light and think that I had just had lunch with Whitey Ashburn, or, I had just watched *Jeopardy* with baseball great Richie Ashburn.

"During one of the conversations, we began talking about the way he wore his baseball cap as a player. The style was a little quirky. There appeared to be a tuck at the front of his hat. As a kid, my friends and I always tried to duplicate the look. It was cool but it wouldn't be cool today. The only way we could come close was to put baseball cards in the inside of the cap under the sweat band. I told Richie how my friends tried to copy his cool look. He told me that was exactly the way he did his hat. Topps, the baseball card company, gave him complimentary cards each spring training. He said he would put the cards in the lining of his hat."

Some of the meetings included Donahue's daughter Caitlin. Jim also calls her Caitie. Richie grew fond of Caitie and would make special shopping trips to an area market for Caitie's lunch.

"We talked a lot about baseball and other subjects but when the subject of the Hall of Fame was mentioned you could tell that Richie cared a lot about being elected. He would joke about the situation but you could tell he felt deeply about not being included in the Hall of Fame. He would say it was no big deal to him, but it was."

After a life time in baseball, Ashburn had little to do in late August and September during the strike season. He wasn't playing and he wasn't going to Veterans Stadium and other

National League ballparks to announce Phillies games. He couldn't even watch a broadcast of another Major League Baseball team.

"At times before the strike, we would get together for lunch when the Phillies were in town. One day I asked to have some items signed for the campaign. I didn't really want to bother him, but he said come on over for lunch. The lunches were more frequent during the strike. We would talk about baseball and our families. Sometimes we talked about events in the news. They were enjoyable conversations with an enjoyable man, Richie Ashburn.

"Several of the occasions I had my younger daughter, Caitie with me. It got to the point that Richie would tell me to make sure Caitie would join them. Richie was a diabetic and he didn't eat all of the sweets sent to him in the television booth by his fans but he was always grateful for the offerings. On the mornings Caitie would join us for lunch, Richie went to the neighborhood farmers' market to get lemonade for Caitie. Here was the guy you heard on the radio and television making a special trip, out of his way, for my daughter. That's the kind of guy Richie was.

"Caitie never got to know her grandfathers. One day she said to me, 'So, that's what it is like having a grandpop.' We have photographs of Richie and Caitie. She was then up to Richie's chest. He was always very kind to Caitie; he took to her.

"In Richie's home, actually in his kitchen, was a portrait of a young girl. For the longest time I never asked Richie about the painting. Several days before Richie was inducted into the Hall of Fame, Caitie and I visited him at lunch. Richie had a legal pad in front of him and he was working on his speech. He said, 'It's good you are here, I need some help.' I thought it was funny that he waited until a week before the ceremony to write his talk. I knew Mike Schmidt had a professional speech writer working with him for his talk at the Hall of Fame. I knew he had been working on the speech for six months.

"He was trying to get his thoughts together and making a list of names of people he wanted to mention. As he was writing he was looking at the portrait of the young woman. He was writing and looking at Caitie and then looking at the portrait.

"Finally, he asked Caitie if she know who was the girl in the portrait. Caitie didn't know. It was Richie's sister Donna. The portrait was painted when Donna was about the same age as Caitie. Donna died of cancer in 1989. That night I told my wife I then understood why Richie took to Caitie. He was always so nice to her."

Richie Ashburn was also kind to Jim Donahue when Jim was caring for his ailing mother. "I was taking care of my mom and at one point I changed my work shifts so I could be home with her during the day. I worked midnights and Richie would adjust the time of our meetings. He would work around my work schedule and the time I needed to take care of my mom."

As the long evenings of the strike came to a conclusion, Jim had a prediction for Richie. "I told him his life would be very different this time next year because he would be in the Hall of Fame."

Indeed, Ashburn's life did change. Before his election a few fans might gather for Ashburn's autograph after a game. When Ashburn became a Hall of Famer, the number of fans waiting for Richie increased to 20 or 30 a night. "Being a Hall of Famer is ruining my life," Richie jokingly commented to people.

Jean Ashburn remembered that her father would always take the time after games to sign autographs for waiting fans. "I remember going to games with him after he was elected," she said. "I would wait in the car after the game concluded as he signed autographs."

* * *

One night Richie Ashburn asked Jim Donahue a pointed question. Ashburn couldn't figure out why Donahue was spending so much of his free time on the Why the Hall Not? campaign. Donahue began collecting signatures at the time the two of them barely knew each other.

Jim recalled, "Richie asked me why was it a big deal for me to have him in the Hall of Fame. I told him that I had played a lot of baseball as a kid. I was in Little League and I played in the neighborhood but I never advanced. I dreamed of being a Major League player and being good enough to be an All Star and play in the World Series. It's every kid's dream to be in the Hall of Fame.

"My career was over as a youngster, the same as most kids. I told Richie that he had progressed so far beyond what I and countless of others had accomplished. He was signed to a professional contract, he made it to the Major Leagues; he was an All Star; he was a batting champion, and he played in the World Series. I told him he made it to an elite level. He played with some of the best players ever to play in the Major Leagues, such as Mickey Mantle, Hank Aaron, Willie Mays and many others. He was a big part of the golden age of baseball players. I told Richie that he deserved to be in the Hall of Fame with those players.

"Richie had a dry wit about him and he said, 'Well, if you put it that way, it is a big deal.'

"'Of course, it is a big deal when you think about it,' I told him."

* * *

As 1995 dawned the strike was in the process of being settled. Jim Donahue had high hopes that 1995 would be the year Richie Ashburn entered the Hall of Fame. Donahue packed up many boxes with signed petitions and postcards urging the Hall of Fame's Veterans' Committee to select Richie. He then shipped them to Cooperstown.

The Philadelphia media continued its coverage. The afternoon show host at WIP radio, Howard Eskin, also paid a lot of attention to the Why the Hall Not? campaign and mentioned the campaign on his show. "Howard would check with me and keep up on the progress of the campaign. Not everyone is a fan of Howard but he does work hard. He follows stories and he does his homework before reporting.

"When I was collecting signatures at the Hall of Fame section of Veterans Stadium, Howard came up to me and harassed me in a good way. He would tell me that Richie would never be in the Hall of Fame. Howard at times makes statements and he knows people will argue with him. I asked if he wanted to make a bet. I told Howard that not only will Richie Ashburn be inducted but he will be there the same day Mike Schmidt, a friend of Howard, goes into Cooperstown and that Richie will steal Mike's thunder. I told Howard I would buy him the best dinner that could be found in Cooperstown if it didn't happen. If Richie made the Hall of Fame, Howard would have to buy me the dinner. Howard said he would never have to pay off on that bet."

The Phillies were also pulling for Richie to become a Hall of Fame member, according to Jim. "I didn't have much contact with the Phillies organization," he said. "Richie told me that the team always felt he should be in the Hall of Fame. Richie's uniform number, 1, had been retired and the Phillies usually only retire numbers of Hall of Fame caliber players."

Richie Ashburn might have harbored doubts about his election, especially after a pre-game television interview he did with Mookie Wilson of the New York Mets. Wilson wore uniform # 1, the same number Ashburn wore as an original Met. Ashburn asked Wilson who was the first Met to wear the # 1. Wilson didn't have a clue that Richie was the original Met # 1.

Hall of Fame

AS THE YEAR 1995 began, Jim Donahue could only sit back and wait to see if the members of the Veterans' Committee would agree with him and thousands of other fans that Richie "Whitey" Ashburn was worthy of a place in baseball's Hall of Fame.

For almost four years, Jim had spent countless hours soliciting signatures for his petitions. He promoted Richie's cause on local and national radio stations and publications. He also deluged Major League Baseball with his petitions and postcards urging the selection of Richie.

Jim believed Richie deserved a place in Cooperstown. Since Steve Carlton had joined the Hall of Fame the previous year, Jim wanted Richie to be inducted with another Phillies' legend, Mike Schmidt.

Schmidt, the slick fielding homerun hitter of the Phillies, was eligible for the first time in 1995. Schmidt didn't have long to wait to see if he would be a first-ballot selection. During the first week of January the Baseball Writers Association of America voted Schmidt into the Hall of Fame. Schmidt received 444 votes or 96.5 percent of the votes cast that year.

"Everyone expected Mike Schmidt to be elected on the first ballot," Jim said. "After his selection, the Hall of Fame ceremony that year had all of the makings of the greatest celebration of all time for Phillies' fans. All that was needed was for the Veterans' Committee to name Richie. We would

know the committee's decision by March. With or without
Richie's election, Mike Schmidt's selection was great for the
fans of Philadelphia. If Richie Ashburn didn't join Schmidt,
it would have been disappointing for me, personally."

* * *

As fans across the country discussed trade rumors during
the winter months of the Hot Stove League and looked forward to another year of baseball, the teams began preparing
for spring training. The announcers, including Richie, also
made their way to Florida.

For Jim Donahue, his task was completed. "My campaign-
ing was done. There was nothing I could do, or other fans
could do, at that point. We just had to wait. Richie was back
on the ballot. I was holding my breath and just hoping for
the best," Jim said.

Jim had an opportunity to speak to Phillies' great and Hall
of Fame pitcher Robin Roberts during that off-season. "Robbie was a teammate of Richie and was a big supporter of his,"
Jim said. "He always thought Richie should have joined him
in the Hall of Fame long before Richie's election."

Roberts began his career with the Phillies in 1948 and
concluded his major league career in 1966. He had a record
of 234 wins and 199 losses for the Phillies and for his career
was 286-245. He also pitched for Baltimore, Houston and the
Chicago Cubs. In 1976, of the 388 votes cast by the baseball
writers for the Hall of Fame, Roberts received 337 votes and
secured his spot in Cooperstown.

"Robbie was a shoe-in," Jim commented. Robin Roberts
deserved a place in Cooperstown.

* * *

Richie went about his life as usual during the early part of
1995. "I talked with Richie several times before the vote was

announced and after Schmidt was elected," Jim said. "He went to Florida early, before the teams arrived for spring training and waited for the season to begin. I talked to him several times by phone. When the conversation turned to the election by the Veterans' Committee, he would only comment that I was a Pollyanna, an eternal optimist."

Larry Shenk of the Phillies had the same type of reaction from Richie that spring. "He did seem resigned to not getting into the Hall of Fame. While in Tampa during the beginning of spring training I asked him where he was going to be the next Tuesday. Hall of Fame announcements are made on Tuesdays. Richie asked me why I thought he was going to be selected since he hadn't had a hit in 35 years."

"Richie was a close friend," Shenk said. "When I joined the Phillies in 1964 Richie was an announcer. I knew him well. We lived in the same development during spring training. Richie was one of a kind."

* * *

As Shenk predicted, the Hall of Fame announced on March 7, 1995, that Richie Ashburn would be inducted in Cooperstown that summer. "A representative of the Hall of Fame asked how to contact Richie. They located him through a sports writer and a press conference was arranged in Tampa," Shenk said. "I hooked up with Richie and I asked him what he thought about the selection. He told me he might not go to Cooperstown. I told him if he doesn't go he would be robbing his family of one of the greatest days of his life."

Shenk said a dinner celebration was held the day of the selection with Richie and members of the Phillies' management. Phillies' broadcaster Chris Wheeler was at the dinner and he believes it was held at the Beachcomber restaurant in Tampa. "There weren't a whole lot of people there. Harry (Kalas) was there, I'm sure. Whitey always acted as if not being in the Hall of Fame was no big deal. But he was more emotional about it than people believed. When he was selected that day, he changed. I think he saw how happy his family was with the selection and it was a big deal, especially for his family."

* * *

Jim Donahue's day began with a family funeral on March 7, 1995. "My wife's great aunt had died and the funeral was in northeast Philadelphia. After the services, we were driving home and I tuned into KYW radio for the traffic report. Before the road report, a reporter said he had big news for Phillies' baseball fans. He said Richie Ashburn was elected to the Hall of Fame. You talk about a change in my emotions. The funeral was a sad event for my family and then the Ashburn election was a joyous one.

"I always believed Richie's election would happen. But it was a dream at times. For four years, I worked on the Why the Hall Not? campaign. I spent a lot of time going to the ballpark to collect signatures, working with reporters and mailing petitions. During the first season, many people were enthusiastic and involved in the campaign and energized. As time went on, people were interested in the campaign and always inquired as to how it was going, but not as actively engaged. I knew the announcement would be made some time in early March but not the exact day. After all that time and work, to actually hear the announcement was a wow moment. It was exhilarating. It is hard to explain my exact feelings."

When Jim returned to his home, he was greeted by a blinking phone-answering machine. He had requests for interviews from newspaper reporters and radio show hosts and congratulations from friends and family.

Jim's answering machine also contained a message from Richie Ashburn—Hall of Famer.

"The message was short and concise," Jim said. "In Richie's usual deadpan voice, he said, 'I guess you heard the news.' He also asked me to call him and I did. Richie was very kind. Richie was elected to the Hall of Fame on the basis of what he did as a player. Richie earned the honor on his own. If what I did helped in any way, I'm honored. I don't want to diminish in any way what Richie accomplished.

"Richie said it was one of the greatest days of his life. Having a small part made all of the work worthwhile to me. I think I was the catalyst for the campaign. I was like the kid with a match walking past an oil refinery. The explosion would happen at some time. I was just in the right place at the right time. I'll admit, at times I thought the campaign might have been a harebrained idea."

One of the first requests for an interview came from Howard Eskin, *WIP* sports radio host. The afternoon of Richie's election, Eskin interviewed Donahue. The next morning Jim was back on WIP talking with the morning crew of Angelo Cataldi, Tony Bruno and Al Morganti. During the show, Donahue gave credit to the WIP hosts, especially Cataldi, for promoting the Why the Hall Not? campaign.

"When I called into the morning show, Angelo talked about Richie's being elected and my campaign. He said he wanted to do something special for me for my four years of hard work. He said I was going to be an honorary judge of the Miss WIP contest, which was taking place at a club on Delaware Avenue in Philadelphia that Friday. One of the other judges was Herb Denenberg, a legendary consumer advocate, newspaper columnist and former Pennsylvania Insurance Commissioner. He had a television segment called Dennenberg's Dump where he trashed products that ripped off consumers. John Bolaris, a television weatherman, and a Miss March from *Playboy* were the other judges. The Miss March was from New Jersey.

"This had to be one of my finest moments. My wife laughed when I told her of my being a judge of a beauty contest. She has a good sense of humor. She has to have one to be married to me. The contest was done in good taste and humor."

The Miss WIP contest wasn't the first live WIP event for Donahue. He said he was a spectator at the station's first Wing Bowl held at the Franklin Plaza Hotel. "The first one had maybe 100 people. Now you need to get a ticket to get into the Wells Fargo Center where the Philadelphia Flyers and 76ers play."

Wing Bowl was started in 1993 by Cataldi and Morganti. The event is held the Friday before Super Bowl Sunday and is billed as a celebration of gluttony. Contestants devour chicken wings to win prizes. Wing Bowl also features women in skimpy costumes. They are dubbed Wingettes.

* * *

George Vecsey of the *New York Times* wrote an article in connection with his Sports of the Times column on March 8, 1995. The headline was: "Better Late Than Never for Ashburn."

The column sums up what at least one baseball expert thought of Richie:

> RICHIE ASHBURN invented Marvelous Marv Throneberry, but that is not the reason he was selected to the Baseball Hall of Fame yesterday. Richie Ashburn also threw Cal Abrams out at home to help the Phillies win the 1950 pennant, which is duly remembered by aging Brooklyn Dodgers fans, but that isn't why Ashburn was selected by the Veterans' Committee, either.
>
> Ashburn was selected because he was just about as good as a center fielder can be, without bashing the ball over the fence 40 times a year. Not every

great center fielder is Willie, Mickey or the Duke, but there should be room in the shrine near the shore of Lake Otesaga for a player who batted .308 over 15 years and ran down most line drives in the power alleys.

Look at this. It is early March, and I take a step out of my house yesterday and the damp, warm, spring-like air goes straight to my head, and all I want to do is write about a combative old cuss I saw playing for the New York Mets in 1962. He played with passion and wit and brains, all three of which went on strike long before the general strike of last August.

Doggone it, I miss baseball. Pro basketball and pro hockey are just lumbering along right now, the dog days, and college basketball is cooking up, and that hideous scab game perpetrated by the Seligs and the Harringtons and the Reinsdorfs does not qualify as baseball.

Baseball is Richie Ashburn slapping foul after foul, waiting for his pitch, wearing out the pitcher. He was reminded of the day when one of his many intentional foul balls struck a woman in the face. The next day he visited her in the hospital, and he apologized for hitting her. 'That isn't the half of it,' she said, adding that while she was being carried out, 'you got me again on the leg.'

Ashburn was proud of the skill, if not the carnage. He could see the frustration in a pitcher's eyes. That's how the game was played then. Nowhere is it written that power is the only criterion for the Hall of Fame, but the Veterans' Committee is there to provide some oversight.

The committee yesterday selected Leon Day, a star of the old Negro Leagues, Vic Willis, a durable

pitcher at the turn of the century, and William Hulbert, who helped organize the National League. By
choosing Ashburn, the committee had to bypass Gil
Hodges, Nellie Fox, Roger Maris and Larry Doby,
but I have no quarrel with the choice of Ashburn.

* * *

Richie Ashburn's election to the Hall of Fame was also a
vindication for Jim Donahue. "Early in the campaign, I heard
a lot of negative comments from people," Jim said. "Some of
them asked what made me think I could pull off the campaign
since I didn't know Richie Ashburn or anyone at the Phillies
or at the Hall of Fame. I always believed in the campaign. I
had to have a positive outlook. If you have a negative attitude,
then what you want won't happen. Some people like to be
negative and some people like to feed off of positive energy.
I was positive when I asked for signatures. I told them it was
their chance to get on the Richie Ashburn bandwagon."

Jim counts his friendship with Richie as one of the positive
outcomes of the campaign.

"Richie Ashburn didn't value things as much as he valued
relationships," Jim said. "One day I was in his kitchen and I
looked at his clock. It was the award he received for being
Rookie of the Year in 1948. It was given to him by the *Sporting News*. Richie said it was a damned good clock and it will
stay where it is as long as it ran and kept time. As soon as it
stopped it was going to be discarded."

Another story Donahue had of how little objects meant to
Richie included the silver bats he won for being the National
League's batting champion in 1955 and 1958. The bats would
bring a lot of money on eBay but Ashburn wasn't even sure
where he stored them, according to Donahue.

"The bats were gifts from the Louisville bat company,"
Jim said. "One day we were having lunch and I asked him

what happened to the bats. I asked Richie, 'Do you have your bats from winning the titles?' Richie said, 'Yeah, probably. I haven't seen them in some time.' Richie suggested we should find them and we went to his basement. He had a dozen or so golf bags stacked against the wall. Every time he went to a golf tournament, someone would give him a bag. Some of them had dish towels draped over them. He started looking in the golf bags and he found the bats. He had stored them there, in the golf bags."

Ashburn's possessions might not have mattered much to him, but friends and heritage did. "In his living room over a couch was a map of the state of Nebraska, his home state. He's the only person I know who has a state map on the living room wall. I asked him about the map one day and he said, 'That's my home state and I'm proud of it.' Richie wasn't pretentious at all. He wore tennis shoes with a hole in the side. He said, 'Why, these are comfortable.' He was going to be who he was. He wasn't going to put on any airs. That is what I admired about him. He was very approachable."

Harry Kalas was Richie Ashburn's long-time friend and television broadcast partner. They worked together for 27 seasons. Kalas had a conversation with Donahue concerning Richie. "We agreed," Donahue recalled. "Richie would always make you feel good about yourself. I would call him and Richie would say, 'Jim Donahue, is this the great Jim Donahue?' I would tell him 'this is the mediocre Jim Donahue.' Richie was just a nice guy.

"I look back and I remember us as two friends having a conversation. We were having lunch together or watching *Jeopardy* as friends. I admired Richie Ashburn. My greatest thrill is to have had Richie Ashburn as a friend. It was my greatest honor when he called me his friend. I don't have a boat load of heroes. Richie is one.

"Richie was a real person. People he touched over the years came to Cooperstown for his induction. He was that kind of guy."

* * *

When the excitement from the announcement of Richie's election to the Hall of Fame faded somewhat, Donahue began making plans to attend the induction ceremony in Cooperstown. He also kept in touch with Richie and Richie's family.

"Karen, Richie's daughter, worked as liaison for the event. Richie couldn't do everything himself. She had a lot of requests for tickets from friends and Richie only had a limited number of tickets. Richie made sure that my wife, daughter and I had tickets. We had VIP tickets and we sat in front during the ceremony. With or without tickets, I was going to be there. I was going to see Richie Ashburn enter the Hall of Fame. It didn't matter if I was in the front seat or back row. I was going to go the year before for the Steve Carlton ceremony but didn't. I swore to myself that I wouldn't go to one until Richie was in the Hall of Fame."

The induction ceremony was set for Sunday, July 30, 1995. Jim and his wife and daughter, Caitie, attended the ceremonies in Cooperstown. Donahue's daughter Heather was away and his son Ryan, who was 19 at the time, had promised some of his friends that he would go with them to Boston. "Ryan decided to spend the time with his friends," Jim said. "I think in hindsight, he was sorry that he didn't attend the Hall of Fame ceremony. This was a once-in-a-lifetime opportunity to be that close to baseball history."

Jim had visited the Hall of Fame in the early 1990's. The 1995 trip would be much more meaningful for him. Donahue was more than a fan; he was the catalyst behind the Why the Hall Not? campaign.

Donahue said he had a "vision" for the Philadelphia celebration at Cooperstown. He believed it would be "cool" to have a Mummers' string band lead the parade out of town on Pioneer Street to Doubleday field. He said the food would also be very Philadelphia, cheese steaks, Tastykakes and soft pretzels. Donahue said he suggested the Philly-themed celebration and Richie liked the idea. "Richie told Bill Giles of the Phillies who also thought it was a good idea," Donahue said. "Giles is known for his promotions at Phillies' games. By the time Giles heard about the idea, it was too late to implement at Cooperstown."

Donahue and his family spent Thursday and Friday before the ceremony enjoying the festive atmosphere in Cooperstown on Hall of Fame weekend. "By Friday, a lot of the fans had arrived along with vendors that sold baseball items to the huge number of fans. There was an outdoor memorabilia market. Joan and I walked the town and I saw many of the people I had met during the campaign and stopped to talk with them.

"Joan commented that I knew a lot of people in Cooperstown. People came up to me to say how happy and proud they were that Richie was going to be in the Hall of Fame. Some of the people had the Ashburn bumper stickers. Some of them even asked me to sign them. On Saturday I was at the swimming pool at the hotel. Joan and Caitie were with me. Someone came up and said, 'You were the guy who did the campaign for Whitey.' He grabbed some of his friends and we began talking about the Ashburn campaign and Richie and baseball. They had a lot of questions about Richie. Joan commented that a quiet day around the pool ended with me holding court.

"I always though Richie would be in the Hall of Fame. I never lost faith but this weekend was the culmination of the long campaign. The weekend was a rewarding, fulfilling and interesting for me."

Saturday was a crazy day in Cooperstown, Jim recalled. "It was like a carnival atmosphere. People were all around town. PRISM, a local network in Philadelphia at the time, was doing some remote broadcasts. Somehow the reporter spotted me in the crowd and I did an interview with him in front of the Hall of Fame."

* * *

Induction day began for Jim and his family with a tour of the Hall of Fame. Ted Spencer, the then curator of the Hall of Fame, was taking a small group on a private walk around the building beginning at 9:00 a.m. On the tour were family members of Richie Ashburn and Mike Schmidt. Some of the Philadelphia Phillies executives and Mayor Ed Rendell were also on the tour, Jim remembers. Jim estimates about 20 people were guided through the Hall of Fame by Spencer.

During the tour, Jim was informed that one of his ideas for the ceremony would take place. "Mayor Rendell told me that the Mummers would be attending," Jim said. "He said some of them were making the trip from Philadelphia and they were bringing their banjos with them to play before the assembled crowd."

* * *

Spencer, who has retired from the Hall of Fame, recalls the turnout for the induction ceremony was even larger than the one in 1999 which featured George Brett, Nolan Ryan and Robin Yount. The Veterans' Committee that year also selected Orlando Cepeda, Nestor Chylak, Frank Selee and Joe Williams. The 1999 class had multiple baseball stars but they didn't outdraw Richie and Mike Schmidt.

"They had 220 buses filled with fans from Philadelphia," Spencer said. "We didn't know how to handle all of the business. We do now. That year served as a model for how we now conduct the weekend."

Spencer was on notice that Philadelphia would have a large turnout for the induction of Richie and Schmidt. "When Schmidt was announced, we received a lot of calls at the Hall of Fame about the ceremony, but when Ashburn was announced we were swamped with calls from his fans."

Richie's induction also gave Spencer a chance to get to know Ashburn and his family. "We had a tremendous relationship.

At first the Hall of Fame couldn't secure any of his material to display. But we worked together and we finally received a number of items to display. When I met him I told him that we planted a lot of peas together. He looked at me quizzically and I explained that in the spring I worked in my garden and as I worked I would listen to him on the radio."

Richie's connection to sports fans, especially young ones, was illustrated by another story related by Spencer that took place in the mid 2000's. "A young boy who probably wasn't even born when Richie died, visited the Hall of Fame and was enamored with Richie. That is what heritage is all about."

* * *

The Otesaga Hotel and Resort was used as a central location for the Hall of Fame players and their families, Jim recalls. The grandness of the hotel was a perfect setting for baseball's elite. The hotel has been a resort since 1909 and is a Federal-style structure with an imposing front portico supported by massive 30-foot columns, The Otesaga occupies 700 feet of lakefront on the southern shore of Lake Otsego. Jim remembers the Otesaga Hotel as a southern-styled mansion in a beautiful setting.

The Donahue family was staying outside of town but attended a few events at the Otesaga Hotel as different receptions and dinners were scheduled during the weekend. They met at the Otesaga to be shuttled to the induction ceremony at Doubleday Field.

"Shuttle buses were running to the field," Donahue said. "We were on a bus with former Phillies' players Von Hayes and Gary Maddox and Bill Giles of the Phillies' management. Joan, Caitie and I were about the last passengers on the bus. I remember former baseball commissioner Bowie Kuhn coming to the bus and knocking on the door to see if a seat was available. There wasn't."

The bus ride only lasted a few minutes as the field was close to the hotel.

"I got off the bus and I'll never forget what I saw," Jim recalled. "There was a sea of red and white, the colors of the Philadelphia Phillies. I remember Bill Giles commenting on all of the red. Richie even alluded to the red in his speech."

The Hall of Fame induction venue includes a VIP seating section and a fenced off area for those attending the event. "Each player only had so many tickets for the VIP event. It wasn't a priority of mine to have a reserved seat but I'm glad my family received them. I was able to take better photographs because of my seating position, but I was just glad to be in Cooperstown to see and hear Richie as he entered the Hall of Fame. Richie was very moved by the honor even though he used the old Groucho Marx gag line that he wouldn't belong to any club that would have the likes of him. At the conclusion of his talk Richie thanked everyone for making it one of the best days of his life. It was obviously a moving experience for Richie. It was a moving experience for me. There were some hot days at Veterans Stadium where I was collecting signatures that I wondered if I was out of my mind. My good late friend, Max Silverman, once told me I was like Don Quixote in that I never give up."

* * *

The Hall of Fame estimated that 28,000 fans were on hand to see Richie inducted into baseball's Hall of Fame. Besides Richie, the Veterans' Committee also selected Leon Day, William Hulbert and Vic Willis for inclusion. The maximum number of players the committee could select was four. Willis was a pitcher in the 1900's, Day played in the Negro Leagues and Hulbert was the founder and second president of the National League.

The Hall of Fame's website reviews the 1995 ceremony and comments on Richie, "A Veterans' Committee selec-

tion, Ashburn was a clutch hitter and solid fielder during his
career, playing mostly for the Philadelphia Phillies. He was
a lifetime .308 hitter and eclipsed the .300 mark in nine of
his 15 seasons. Ashburn amassed 2,574 hits, twice captured
the National League batting title and was selected to five All-
Star teams. Ashburn quickly moved to the broadcast booth
following his playing days and called Phillies games for more
than three decades."

As for Schmidt, the Hall of Fame comments, "Schmidt
captured 96.5 percent of the BBWAA's (Baseball Writers
Association of America) 460 ballots in his first year of eligibility. Utilizing a rare combination of power and defense
to become one of the best third basemen in baseball history,
Schmidt smashed 548 home runs during an 18-year career.
He belted 40 home runs or more in three separate seasons and
hit 30 or more home runs ten other times. His 48 home runs
during the 1980 season established a Major League record for
third basemen. In a game against the Chicago Cubs in 1976,
Schmidt hit home runs in four consecutive at bats. The twelve-
time All-Star was a three-time National League MVP, won
ten Gold Gloves and was named *The Sporting News* Player of
the Decade for the 1980s."

Richie Ashburn's Hall of Fame plaque says:

DON RICHARD ASHBURN
(RICHIE)
Philadelphia, N.L., 1948-1959
Chicago, N.L., 1960-1961
New York, N.L., 1962
Durable, Hustling Lead-Off Hitter and
Clutch Performer with Superb Knowledge of
Strike Zone. Batted .308 Lifetime with Nine
.300 Seasons and 2,574 Hits in 2,189 Games,
Winning Batting Championships in 1955 and

1958. As a Center Fielder, Established Major
League Records for Most Years Leading League
in Chances (9), Most Years 500 or More Putouts
(4) and Most Seasons 400 or More Putouts (9).

* * *

Induction day was rewarding and also draining for Jim
Donahue. "When Richie started his speech, the reality started
to set in for me. That's when my emotions started. It was a very
long ceremony, maybe three hours with all of the inductions
and speeches. I remember admiring Richie's mother. She sat
through the whole ceremony. We all baked in that sun for
three hours. It shows in the photographs taken of me that
day. My face is very red."

After the induction ceremony, Jim, his family and others
returned to the Otesaga Hotel for receptions and dinners. "A
reception for Richie and his family members was taking place
in Richie's mother's room. Joan and I were asked to attend and
we took the elevator to the floor but decided not to intrude on
the family celebration."

As Joan and Jim turned to depart, Richie Ashburn was
exiting the elevator. Ashburn approached Jim and made a
statement that surprised Jim.

"Richie said, 'Jimmy, I'm so sorry. I hope you will forgive
me.' I asked, 'For what?' Richie said he had planned to mention me and his niece Claire in his speech and the Why the
Hall Not? campaign. Richie said as soon as he began talking
about his daughter Jan he lost his concentration on his notes.
You could tell Richie was emotional when he mentioned his
deceased daughter. I told Richie that he had thanked his fans
and I consider myself one of his fans. That was all I was from
the beginning of the campaign, a fan."

Joan Donahue then suggested that Richie and her husband
pose for a photograph with Ashburn's Hall of Fame plaque.

Richie readily agreed. The photograph is a prized Donahue possession.

While at the Otesaga Hotel, Donahue said he also had his first face-to-face encounter with Ed Stack, President of the Hall of Fame. According to Jim, Richie introduced him to Stack by saying, "Hi Ed, do you known my friend Jim Donahue?" Jim recalled. "Ed Stack said, 'Sounds familiar.' I told him I was the one who sent him all of those petitions and postcards. He said, 'Oh, that Jim Donahue. I guess you are very happy today.' We were all very happy that day."

As a baseball fan, Jim was in his glory. Everywhere he looked he saw the stars of the game. He was allowed to take a group photo of the assembled baseball greats. "It was amazing," Donahue said. "There were more than thirty Hall of Fame members sitting in the stands of the stadium. The seats were just like a high school football stadium. They were assembled for a group shot. I had my camera and the Hall of Fame photographer recognized that I was a friend of Richie Ashburn. He told me I could take my own photograph as long as I didn't get in his way. Usually, only the official photographer is allowed to take photographs. To see them all assembled was glorious for a fan."

Joan Donahue didn't recognize the Hall of Fame players by sight at the Otesaga Hotel, but she did spot actor Paul Gleason who had been in more than 100 television episodes and movies during his career, including *Trading Places*. "Joan didn't know Yogi Berra but she knew Paul Gleason," Jim Donahue said. "Paul approached me and asked if I was a friend of Richie Ashburn. He had Hall of Fame postcards. He was a collector of memorabilia and he wanted me to see if Richie would sign them for him.

"I told Paul I would see if Richie would sign them if Paul did me a favor. I told him my wife was sitting by herself and didn't really know anyone at the reception. I told him if he would go and talk with Joan, I would see if Richie would sign his postcards. Richie signed them and I also got a photo for Paul.

"Paul was a very nice guy. He said he hoped we would run into each other at some of the ball yards across the nation. He was there with some of the Boston Red Sox people. He was a fan."

Richie Ashburn wasn't through signing items. He also autographed a Hall of Fame baseball for Donahue's daughter, Caitie. "Richie said Mike Schmidt also should sign Caitie's baseball," Jim said. "Schmidt wasn't signing many items that day. Schmidt and his family were sitting on a bench in the lake area. Richie took Caitie by the hand and led her to Schmidt. Richie said, 'Schmitty, you need to sign this ball for my girlfriend. Mike said sure and he signed. Richie did something special for Caitie."

Jim added to his collection of Richie Ashburn memorabilia. He had a bumper sticker signed by Richie. "Richie asked if I minded if he signed the bumper sticker to 'my good friend, Jim.' I said I would be honored. It meant a lot to me. I have some of Richie's pipes and golf caps. The pipes are in a zip-lock bag and to this day it still has the tobacco smell. The items create a nice memory for me. When I have a bad day, I look at the collection. It brings back my having lunch with Richie. It's my own little therapy."

On Sunday evening, the Hall of Fame members had their own private dinner. Jim said he had the opportunity to spend a little time with Richie's mother, Genevieve Toots Ashburn. "To this day, she is in my memory," Jim said.

On induction day, Toots Ashburn was quoted in a newspaper article. She commented on Richie as a youngster. She said, "He'd throw the ball up, hit it and used the three little trees in the yard for bases. My husband said he had a natural talent. In winter when it was too cold to play outside, he would throw the ball against a wall in the house. I told him to stop because it would ruin the wallpaper but he never paid me any attention."

Jim concluded the day with a dinner in a local restaurant. He spotted Howard Eskin, the WIP radio afternoon man. Eskin visited with Donahue and his family. On his radio show, Eskin had bet Donahue a dinner in Cooperstown if Richie was inducted the same day as Mike Schmidt. "I never expected Eskin to pay off the bet. Making the ridiculous wagers was all part of the fun of the show.

"Sunday was an exhausting day. It was a fantastic weekend but it wasn't over. Some of us met in the lobby of the hotel to talk about the day's events before heading back to our rooms for some rest."

On Monday Richie Ashburn did a public signing as one of the newest members of the Hall of Fame. Later in the day the annual Hall of Fame game took place. That year the teams were the Detroit Tigers and Chicago Cubs. Richie and Mike Schmidt threw out the first ball. Jim and his family stayed for the game before returning to Philadelphia the next day.

"Wow, what an incredible weekend," Jim recalled. "It was overwhelming to me. It was gratifying that some people believe I had something to do with Richie's election, but I didn't. He was elected on his skills and his record as a major leaguer. He had thousands and thousands of fans like me. He was such a great, down-to-earth person. He was the same in person as he was broadcasting a game."

With the end of the Why the Hall Not? campaign, Jim felt a letdown. "When one of the Phillies' official photographers took a photo of Richie and his Hall of Fame plaque, I was shaking and misting up. The reality was hitting me that something positive had came out of the campaign. Richie's entering the Hall of Fame with Mike Schmidt was exactly what I had imaged years before at the Woodbine Inn. Actually, the ceremony was better than I even imagined. It couldn't have been more perfect. I was glad Richie lived to see the induction. Some players have been elected after their deaths. The ceremony wouldn't have been the same without Richie."

The day after driving back from Cooperstown Jim was back to work. "I guess that first day at work felt like strolling down Main Street after climbing Mount Everest," he said.

A Hall of Fame Life

RICHIE ASHBURN WAS a member of the most elite club in baseball, the Hall of Fame. For years, he felt he was destined to be locked out of Cooperstown. Richie joked during television broadcasts of Phillies games after his induction that he now deserved some respect from his broadcasting partner Harry Kalas. When someone suggested his election to the Hall of Fame validated his career, Richie is quoted as saying, "My career doesn't need validation."

Richie did display some resentment about the length of time needed for him to gain admittance to the Hall of Fame. He said, "I feel fortunate to receive the honor but they didn't carry me in on sedan chairs." One Ashburn family member recalled Richie's eyes dancing when he learned of his Hall of Fame selection.

Richie recalled being asked how it felt be an institution in Philadelphia. He replied, "I want to be one before I got into one; it was a close race, believe me." He always did say that playing in Philadelphia was one of the best things to happen to him.

Another line Richie often used was being a member of the Hall of Fame had ruined his life because of all of the extra demands on his time.

Not so.

Richie remained the same easy-going person. His daughter Jean Ashburn remembered attending Phillies games with her father after his election to the Hall of Fame. Jean recalled sitting in the car waiting for her father after the game had concluded. Richie would spend whatever time necessary signing autographs for waiting fans.

"Dad was so nice to fans," Jean Ashburn said. "It didn't matter if you were his daughter or a stranger. He was never grumpy to the end. He would stop and sign autographs."

* * *

While Richie Ashburn remained the same Nebraska country gentleman he was before his induction, his life did become more hectic, according to Jim Donahue.

"As a Hall of Famer, Richie was asked to do personal appearances," Jim said. "When the team was on the road, he was always being interviewed or asked to stop by a sports memorabilia show. It was nice for Richie and it definitely changed his life. When the All-Star game came to Philadelphia in 1996, Richie was a spokesman for the Fanfest activities. He was Richie Ashburn, Hall of Famer. He always seemed to enjoy people asking for his autograph. He would sign items and add HOF 95, for the year he entered the Hall."

What didn't change were Jim's lunches with Richie. Those lunch meetings continued between the two friends, usually during off days for the Phillies. The conversations always revolved around family, friends, world events and, of course, baseball.

During one of those meetings, Richie presented Donahue with a signed lithograph done by artist Stan Kotzen. "Stan had sent a batch of the lithographs to Richie to sign. They were sitting on a love seat. Richie said he would get one for me. I had already ordered one from Stan but I didn't want to say no to Richie. Richie started to sign one and ashes from his pipe blew on the top one. 'Well, you don't want that one,' Richie said. He signed the next one with a Sharpie and gave it to me. I believe the rest were signed in pencil.

"I later ran into Stan and he said he had saved the first print for me. I have the signed prints. They are some of the items I keep. I have another signed charcoal sketch of Richie. I actually have a family room in my home where I have all of my Richie Ashburn material. Joan says it is the shrine to Saint Richie."

* * *

The Why the Hall Not? campaign had successfully concluded, but Jim received inquiries concerning his future plans. Would he conduct another campaign for another deserving player? The name of former Philadelphia Phillies and Cincinnati Reds star Pete Rose come up in a number of conversations.

Rose was one of baseball's brightest stars for more than two decades, beginning in the 1960's. He won a Rookie of the Year award, was an All Star multiple times and a league Most Valuable Player. Rose was known for his hustle on the ball field. He was called Charlie Hustle. Rose collected more than 4,000 hits during his career.

Rose's statistics easily qualify him for a place in the Hall of Fame but his off-field betting activities on baseball gained him a lifetime ban in 1989. Rose at first denied betting on baseball but admitted doing so while he was managing the Reds.

"Some people wanted to know about my next campaign," Jim said. "I was getting calls and people at the Cooperstown celebration asked the question about my next one. Some people wanted to know if I would work to get Pete Rose elected. Also, the grandson of Danny Murtaugh wrote to help get Danny into the Hall of Fame."

Murtaugh was born in Chester, Pennsylvania, close to where Jim lives. Murtaugh was a major league second baseman but gained fame for his managing. He guided two Pittsburgh Pirate teams to World Series victories.

"I said no. The work I did on behalf of Richie Ashburn was a labor of love," Jim said. "It was a tremendous sacrifice on the part of my wife and my whole family. Joan deserves more credit than I do. I worked during the week and spent many weekends at Veterans Stadium collecting signatures. Many believed I was acting on a pie-in-the-sky vision. I'd envisioned the Hall of Fame ceremony with Richie but I've envisioned a lot of things in my life that never materialized.

"I had jumped back into the real world after Cooperstown."

* * *

Fans across the Delaware Valley continued to listen to the Hall of Fame announcer during the Phillies' season. The Hall of Fame election didn't alter Richie's lifestyle. He worked at his job announcing, he exercised and he tried to keep his diabetes in check.

On Monday, September 8, 1997, Richie was in the broadcasting booth as the Philadelphia Phillies played in New York against the Mets. Richie's first team as a major league player was the Phillies and his final major league team was the Mets. The Phillies drubbed the Mets 13-4 that night. Mike Grace was the winning pitcher. Third baseman Scott Rolen led the offense for the Phillies with a home run and three RBIs. The win didn't improve the Phillies' season much, as the team was more than 30 games behind the league leaders in fifth place in the standings.

The game would be the last one called by the Hall of Fame's Richie Ashburn. Ashburn had voiced a fear of dying while on the road. Richie did die the next morning in the Grand Hyatt Hotel in New York City.

In the early morning hours, Richie complained of chest pains and contacted Eddie Ferenz, the Phillies' traveling secretary. The *Philadelphia Inquirer* reported, Ferenez summoned the Phillies' trainer, Jeff Cooper. By 5:00 a.m., Hall of Fame member Richie Ashburn was dead. The headline on the story written by Frank Fitzpatrick was: "A Phillie for the ages, Richie Ashburn dies."

"The broadcaster and Hall of Fame centerfielder, 70, apparently had a heart attack in a New York hotel," the story stated. "Young, blonde and fast as a deer, he was the city's favorite Phillie though out the 1950's. And for the last 35 years, even on the night he died, Richie Ashburn's voice, as flat as his beloved Nebraska, meant summer to a million Philadelphians." The story quotes former player and broadcaster Tim McCarver as saying, "I don't think it's overstating it at all to say that Philadelphia has lost its most well-loved sports hero ever." McCarver began his broadcasting career with the Phillies and once played for the Phillies.

The word of Ashburn's death spread through the Phillies' organization. Ruly Carpenter Jr., former Phillies' owner, recalled fishing in a pond early in the morning of Tuesday, September 9. When he saw someone rushing towards him, he knew the news was not good.

Larry Shenk, Phillies publicity director, worked early in the day gathering information to issue a news release on Richie's death. The release issued on Tuesday, September 9, 1997, over Shenk's name read:

> EDITORS NOTE: We've just learned of Richie Ashburn's death this morning in New York. We'll have more details as the day progresses and will get back to you. We'll also attempt to come up with tributes from his many teammates, friends, etc.)
>
> Richie Ashburn, an icon in Phillies' baseball history, died early Tuesday morning in his room at the Grand Hyatt Hotel in New York, the ballclub announced. He died of an apparent heart attack.
>
> Ashburn, 70, broadcast his final game on Monday night at Shea Stadium, a 13-4 Phillies win over

the Mets. Ironically, Ashburn's Hall of Fame career began with the Phillies and ended with the Mets in 1962. He joined the Phillies broadcast team the following year.

Ashburn, a speedy center fielder, broke in with the Phillies in 1948. He hit .333 and was named the National League Rookie Of The Year. He spent 12 years with the Phillies and was a member of the 1950 National League champion Whiz Kids. His throw home cut down a Brooklyn Dodgers runner with the potential winning run and paved the way for the Phillies extra-inning win which vaulted them into the World Series against the New York Yankees.

During his Phillies career, Ashburn won two batting titles, .338 in 1955 and .350 in 1958. He finished second three times. He led the National League in hits and triples three times and walks and runs scored, four times.

Defensively, he led NL outfielders in putouts nine times, tying a ML record for most years leading outfielders in putouts.

A six-time All-Star, Ashburn was traded to the Chicago Cubs after the 1959 season. He played with the Cubs in 1960 and 1961. Ashburn completed a 15-year career with the expansion New York Mets in 1962.

During his career he hit over .300 nine times and compiled a .308 batting average. In 2, 189 games, he collected 2,574 hits.

In addition to playing and broadcasting, Ashburn reached thousands of lives as a columnist with the old *Philadelphia Bulletin* and *Philadelphia Daily News*.

Ashburn was named the Philadelphia Sportscaster of the year in 1991.

He achieved baseball's highest honor when he was elected to the Baseball Hall of Fame in 1995.

Ashburn was born in Tilden, NE, March 19, 1927.

— *Larry Shenk*

* * *

Shenk had little difficulty compiling words of praise for Richie Ashburn's life from his fellow teammates and friends. Before the day was concluded, the Phillies had distributed two sets of tributes. The tributes included:

"Richie was a very special and unique friend who loved his wonderful family so very much. Loved people, loved the game of baseball and loved his Phillies. His fantastic sense of humor and ability to make people smile and be happy was so wonderful. All who knew him will miss him tremendously. My wife Nancy and I send our prayers and sympathy to his beloved family and many friends."

— *Bill Giles, Phillies' Chairman*

"Richie Ashburn was a Phillies' treasure. He made baseball fun for Phillies' fans. He was 'special' as a player, broadcaster, person and friend. Richie was #1 as a player and #1 represents what he was to the hearts of millions of Phillies fans."

— *David Montgomery, Phillies' President*

"Not only was he a Hall of Famer, but he was a true gentleman. It won't be the same without him."

— *Lee Thomas, Phillies' Senior Vice President and Phillies' General Manager*

"He was like a brother to me. Truly one of my best friends in life. Richie was a joy to be around for 27 years. Not only for his baseball expertise but for his wonderful sense of humor. He will be greatly missed."

— *Harry Kalas, Phillies' Broadcaster*

"I've always felt fortunate to work with him and to have him as a friend. I always thought that we all work well together and he was the main reason for that."

— *Chris Wheeler, Phillies' Broadcaster*

"Nicole and I are just devastated. Whitey always went out of his way for us. He earned tremendous respect throughout his life on and off the field. Respect that not many people can match. He was a joy to be around because he always had a smile and a story to be told. We truly feel as if we lost part of our family. Our prayers go out to his family and many friends and his buddies in the booth."

— *Darren and Nicole Daulton (Daulton was a Phillies' catcher.)*

"This is a sad day for the Phillies and their fans. We have lost a cherished friend. For 50 years Whitey Ashburn had been a part of the daily lives of Philadelphians through the spring and summer months. You don't have to know him personally to consider him a friend. I will always remember Whitey as a gifted broadcaster, a gin rummy partner, a golfing buddy, a supporter of my career, a deserving Hall of Famer, and most of all, a good friend. On behalf of the Schmidts, I would like to extend our sympathy to the Ashburn family and friends."

— Mike Schmidt

"Some people you look at as indestructible, Richie was one of those people. He improved with age. No matter how he aged he excelled at everything he did. I tried to beat him in golf, tennis, and squash and I couldn't do it. I just think he was one of the most unique men I've ever known. I feel for his entire family."

—Jim Bunning, Congressman, Kentucky,
Former Phillie and Hall of Fame Pitcher

"He was probably one of the most lovable and wittiest figures I've ever been around. I have so many fond memories of him and all the laughs we shared. It was like he was part of your family, he was such a big part in all our lives."

—Jim Fregosi, Former Phillies' Manager

"He was a great man. I was associated with him for so many years. He was so good to me. I enjoyed being around him and talking baseball. I will miss him. A lot of people will miss him."

— Tony Taylor, Former Phillie Player.

"I've known him ever since he broke in with the Phillies. I remember him as the centerfielder with The Whiz Kids. You could talk about Richie Ashburn forever. Baseball is much poorer today because he is not with us. He has a mother in Nebraska. And everyday when he'd be in Chicago, he'd say to me,

'Say something to my mother.' I'd always say hello
for him because she'd always tune in our telecasts."
— *Harry Carey, Chicago Cubs' Broadcaster*

* * *

While Larry Shenk was busy compiling additional tributes
for Richie Ashburn, fan Jim Donahue learned of the death
of his friend.

"My wife and I were at Cape May on Tuesday for a long
weekend. It was our 25th wedding anniversary on September
9," Jim said. "I was planning to return home on Wednesday.
Richie's son had called my home and wanted to contact me
to tell me of his father's death. My son Ryan called me to tell
me of the bad news.

"The previous night I had listened to him on television. The
Phillies were playing the Mets. His death was more than a
shock. After I talked with Ryan, I heard about Richie on the
television news. About an hour later a *Daily News* reporter
called me for comments. Fox News also contacted me. They
were coming to New Jersey to interview Bill Campbell and
wanted to know if I would also be interviewed. I didn't really
want to do it but they said it wouldn't take too long. All I
wanted to do was to have a quiet anniversary dinner. The
interview took 90 minutes for my ten seconds of the segment."

"When my son called, I was very upset, obviously. My father
had died November 1994, before Richie went into the Hall
of Fame. I remembered going to the ballpark with my dad
to watch Richie. Those trips were part of our father and son
relationship. I remember telling my wife that with Richie's
passing this part of life was closed.

"My daughter Caitie was close to Richie and his death
affected her. It was a very emotional day. The rest of the day
was a blur. We decided to pack and leave Cape May early."

* * *

As reporters were preparing to ask Donahue for comments, Shenk released the second of a list of tributes for Ashburn. Richie's death resulted in a flood of tributes from fans, players and many others who knew. What follows is a sample of those.

"I am proud to be on a Phillie Hall of Fame team with him. I admired him most for his courage and truthfulness. It is a loss of a good friend.
— *Dick Allen, Former Phillies' Player*

"He was just super . . . just to see him in center field was great. He ran down a lot of my mistakes. 'Just keep it in the ballpark' they used to tell me and he'll catch it. I'm responsible for him being in the Hall of Fame because he caught so many balls that I gave up. You knew you would get 27 outs out of Richie. He will be missed."
— *Bubba Church, Former Phillies' Player*

"Outside of being a great ballplayer, he was a great fella. He was a fun guy, very personable and a hell of a good ballplayer. One of the best leadoff men I've ever seen. When he got in the field it was all business.
— *Jimmy Bloodworth, Former Phillies' Player*

"We are deeply saddened to learn of this news. Richie's engaging personality touched so many people over the years. As a member of the Hall of Fame family, he will be missed by all of us."
— *Donald C. Marr, Jr., President, Hall of Fame.*

"He was a Hall of Fame player and a Hall of Fame guy. Everyone liked Whitey. "The only time he irritated you was when you were the opposing catcher and he would hit a ball down the left field line—if he didn't turn the hit into a double, he would steal second and then it would be a double anyway.

"I'm going to miss him."

— *Joe Garagiola (Former Major League Player)*

"Richie was originally a catcher, on two occasions while in the minors (on a bunt play) he beat the pitcher and runner to first base and took the throw from the first baseman. Also while in the minors he had seven infield hits in one double-header. He was probably one of the fastest runners I've ever seen in the game.

"I'll miss him as a person; he was a tremendous guy very down to earth. He was a competitor, boy he loved to compete."

— *Maje McDonnell, Former Phillies' Coach and Long-Time Employee*

"I first met Whitey during that spring training in Clearwater. We were roommates in the old Phoenix Hotel. Whitey was our catalyst on offense and our secretary of defense. He was as good a centerfielder as I've seen. Might have been the greatest competitor I've seen. We'll all miss him very much."

— *Robin Roberts (Former Phillies' pitcher and member of the Hall of Fame)*

"I've been fortunate to be around Whitey. He and I are both competitors and I'll never forget the tennis matches we had in spring training. It was only a couple of years ago he ran me around the

court. I can still hear him say, 'Pal, that was two inches outside the line.' I'm with all the thousands of fans who will dearly miss him.'
        — *Lenny Dykstra (Former Phillies' Player)*

"Whitey was special to all of us. I first got to know him in my first spring training back in 1956 and we became good friends for life. He really was a competitor and I loved him because of that. We and thousands of Phillies fans will miss him dearly."
        — *Dallas Green (Former Phillies' Manager)*

"He was a man who loved the Phillies, loved the game, which always meant a lot of me. He was so much fun to be around. You couldn't help to love his dry, midwestern humor."
        — *Paul Owens (Phillies' Executive)*

"He was such a great guy to be taken away from us like this. He was the fiercest competitor I've ever seen. When a pitcher got him out, he hated that pitcher. He wanted to get right back out there and face him again. He couldn't believe he got him out. And on defense, I couldn't remember a ball going over his head.

"He was a job to be around, keeping you loose, keeping you happy. I know I'm gonna miss him. . . . He was never out of character. He was always Richie Ashburn. No matter where you saw him."
        — *Andy Seminick, Former Phillie Player*

"He was a competitor. I roomed with him for eight years, five in Philly and three in the minors.

I named my son after him. Hell of a ballplayer. He was the best leadoff man you ever saw. The tougher the pitcher got, the more he would bear down. I'm still in shock."

— *Putsy Caballero, Former Phillie Player*

"I've known him since I was eight or nine years old. I've always considered him a friend and not an employee. He was a great ballplayer and a very good broadcaster. His sense of humor was priceless. Last I saw Whitey was in August. He's still after my family; claims he was shortchanged by $50 in his 1948 minor league contract. He said with interest and everything, we owe him something like $9.000. You don't find people like Richie Ashburn. My family and I are blessed to have known him."

— *Ruly Carpenter, Former Phillies' Owner*

"Our telecasts will never be the same without Richie. He had great knowledge of the game and mixed it with a warm, wonderful sense of humor."

— *Randy Smith, Executive Vice President and General Manager WB17 (television station)*

EDITOR'S NOTE: This concludes the Ashburn tribute quotes. Complete details regarding funeral arrangements, survivors, etc., probably won't be known until Wednesday morning. We'll be back in touch with everyone again on Wednesday. If there is any change tonight, I'll be in touch with everyone.

— *Larry Shenk*

* * *

Buster Olney of the *New York Times* was one of the first reporters to write about Richie after his death. The story also shows the sadness many felt that night at Shea Stadium as the Phillies team continued its series with the Mets. His story appeared on the day after Richie died and had the headline: "Ashburn Provided Hits, and Humor." Olney's story:

> Richie Ashburn is in the Hall of Fame for his 2,574 hits, 2 batting titles and .308 lifetime batting average. But the longtime Phillies player and broadcaster, who died yesterday after an apparent heart attack, was remembered by friends for his ability to generate laughter.
>
> The Mets broadcaster Bob Murphy remembered that it was Ashburn, 70, who spent his last season as a member of the legendary 1962 Mets, who gave Marv Throneberry the nickname, Marvelous.
>
> Phillies pitcher Curt Schilling joked loudly with Ashburn about whether Schilling, who leads the majors in strikeouts, had enough stuff to strike out Ashburn, one of the game's great contact hitters in his time.
>
> "I know I never could've done it," Schilling said softly yesterday at Shea Stadium before the Phillies played the Mets.
>
> Tim McCarver, an analyst for Mets television broadcasts, shared a broadcast booth with Ashburn when he first began in the business. Ashburn asked him directly and on the air, "Are you nervous?"
>
> "Baseball lost its Will Rogers," McCarver said yesterday.
>
> Schilling added: "When you hear Richie Ashburn's name, you think Phillies. Baseball can't

afford to lose its vessels of good faith, and he was certainly that."

Harry Kalas, who shared his Phillies broadcast booth with Ashburn, said: "He was Mr. Baseball in Philadelphia; he was always so gracious with fans. They'd come up, asking for autographs. He'd sign all the time, saying, 'I'll waive my usual honorarium.'

During Monday's game at Shea, Philadelphia pinch-hitter Kevin Jordan - who, like Ashburn, is from Nebraska - fouled off 10 straight pitches before lining a two-run double. Kalas recalled that Ashburn took particular delight in the at-bat - when Ashburn played, he had played like that.

The Mets broadcaster Ralph Kiner said, "He was the Tony Gwynn of his time."

Shea Stadium's flag flew at half-staff, and there was a moment of silence before the game. The Phillies will honor Ashburn at Veterans Stadium tomorrow, draping black around his No. 1, which is retired.

The sadness of his friends faded when they would tell stories of his humor. McCarver remembered a time when he was ready to quit golf, frustrated by his play. Ashburn loaned him his spare set of clubs, with the word "Whitey" on the head covers. McCarver's golf skills and his love for the game were reborn, and he asked Ashburn if he would part with the clubs.

"Pal, you don't seem to realize I'm attached to these clubs," Ashburn told McCarver, explaining that the Phillies gave him the clubs on a day the team honored him. "They have a certain emotional value for me."

McCarver said, "I'll give you $300 for them."

Ashburn replied, "So much for emotion." McCarver walked away with the clubs and another memory of baseball's Will Rogers.

The *New York Times* on September 10, 1997, ran a story with the headline: "Richie Ashburn, Whiz Kid and Original Met, dies at 70." The story recalled Richie giving Marv Throneberry his nickname. The two had adjoining lockers. "When reporters came around to ask about Throneberry's latest mishap, Ashburn would call him 'marvelous.' Thus was born the legend of Marvelous Marv.

The article also recounted Richie's trouble communicating with the team's shortstop, the Venezuelan-born Elio Chacon, when the two converged on fly balls. Richie "asked the bilingual Joe Christopher how to say 'I got it' in Spanish. Christopher told Ashburn, 'Yo lo tengo.' The next game, Ashburn ran in for a pop-up yelling, 'Yo lo tengo.' Chacon backed off, but Ashburn had neglected to tell left fielder Frank Thomas in on the dialogue. Thomas, who spoke no Spanish, promptly flattened Ashburn."

The story concludes, "To be voted the most valuable player on the worst team in the history of major league baseball is a dubious honor, to be sure," he once observed. "But I was awarded a 24-foot boat equipped with a galley and sleeping facilities for six. After the season ended, I docked the boat in Ocean City, NJ, and it sank."

* * *

The *Philadelphia Inquirer* reported on Richie's death in an article written by Frank Fitzpatrick. The headline was: "A Phillie for the ages, Richie Ashburn dies."

The story reported, "The broadcaster and Hall of Fame centerfielder, 70, apparently had a heart attack in a New York hotel. Philadelphia has lost its most well-loved sports hero ever," one colleague said.

"Young, blonde and fast as a deer, he was the city's favorite Phillie though out the 1950s. And for the last 35 years, even on the night he died, Richie Ashburn's voice, as flat as his beloved Nebraska, meant summer to a million Philadelphians."

A Final Tribute

FAMILY AND FRIENDS, including thousands and thousands of Phillies' fans, were expected to pay a final emotional tribute to All-Star Richie Ashburn. One of the first considerations was to find a place large enough to hold a public visitation. A small church wouldn't be large enough for Philadelphia's all-time favorite athlete.

The location selected for the public ceremony was Memorial Hall at 42nd Street and Parkside Avenue in Philadelphia's Fairmount Park. The Phillies contacted City of Philadelphia officials and the hall was offered. The hall was constructed in connection with the 1876 Centennial Exposition and designed by Hermann J. Schwarzmann. Memorial Hall was one of the nation's first examples of Beaux-Arts architecture and cost $1.5 million to build. The building is 365 feet by 210 feet. President Ulysses S. Grant led the dedication ceremony.

Every inch of the Grand Hall was needed as thousands of people attended the viewing and walked by the casket. One estimate of the attendance was 40,000. The lines were long even before the official start of the service, former Philadelphia Mayor and former Pennsylvania Governor Ed Rendell noted. The Grand Hall was filled with Richie Ashburn fans for many hours.

Chris Wheeler recalled that "the entire 1997 team attended in full uniform, saluting one of their own." Wheeler credits Richie with giving him the chance to broadcast Phillies' games. Wheeler's first time behind the microphone was unexpected. The Phillies were playing the Montreal Expos in a doubleheader and clinched the pennant with a first-game win. Wheeler was working for Larry Shenk in the Phillies' public relations office at the time. As the second game started, according to Wheeler, Richie decided to take the rest of the afternoon off from his broadcasting duties. Wheeler said Richie told him, "'Wheels, I know you've always wanted to do this, so I'm going to take off and leave you here to work with Harry,' Pure Ashburn."

* * *

Larry Shenk of the Phillies issued a press release regarding the funeral arrangements on Wednesday, September 10, 1997, as promised. The press release invited friends and family to Memorial Hall from 11:00 a.m. until 7:00 p.m. on Friday, September 12.

The press release listed survivors as Richie's wife, "Herberta C. Ashburn; daughters Jean M. Ashburn, Sue Ann and (husband) Wayne Morrison; Karen A. and (husband) Bob Hall; sons, Richie E. and (wife) Lisa; John C. and (wife) Mary Ann; mother, Genevieve Warner Ashburn; brother, Robert, sister, Bette Cram; and nine grandchildren."

Contributions were to be sent to the Phillies Charities, Inc., in memory of Richie Ashburn. The donations were distributed to four charities: Jan Ashburn Memorial Fund, Handicapped Boy Scouts of America, Salvation Army and the Philadelphia Orchestra.

The press release also noted that the funeral service and burial were to be private.

* * *

Instead of a lunch on Thursday with Richie, Jim Donahue was preparing to attend the public viewing on Friday. He intended to honor the family's request for a private funeral service and told Richie's daughter Karen that he would do so. Karen told Donahue that he was welcomed at the funeral service. "The church was filled," Donahue recalled. "After the church service, a reception was held at a Philadelphia country club.

Jim recalls Mayor Rendell giving a very emotional speech and mentioning a transistor radio left by one fan at the casket. That radio symbolized the link between Richie and thousands of fans throughout the Delaware Valley, according to Jim and Rendell.

Richie's legacy was one of wit, comfort and joy, Harry Kalas said at the service. He concluded with, "God bless you pal."

Richie Ashburn was buried at the Gladwyne United Methodist Church in Montgomery County, Pennsylvania.

* * *

The church services inspired one fan, Chuck Brodsky to write a song about Richie. Brodsky, who lives in Ashville, North Carolina, and has recorded other baseball-themed lyrics, recorded the song *Whitey & Harry*. The song recalls listening to "Whitey" Ashburn and Harry Kalas on the radio and how he misses Richie.

* * *

The Philadelphia Phillies continue to honor Richie Ashburn. Citizens Bank Park was opened in south Philadelphia on April 12, 2004. The 43,500-seat ballpark has a number of reminders of Richie. There was fan support to name the stadium after Richie.

A larger-than-life bronze statue occupies a portion of Ashburn Alley, an interactive memorial for fans. Harry Kalas said Ashburn Alley is a place to have fun and Richie would have liked that. Ashburn Alley is located just beyond center field, Richie's position for many years.

In 2008 the Phillies also released a DVD titled *Richie Ashburn: A Baseball Life*. The DVD was narrated by Harry Kalas and produced by Dan Stephenson of the Phillies. Kalas said be believed Richie would have liked Ashburn Alley and it will keep "Whitey's spirit alive" for generations.

"I started working for the Phillies in 1982 and the job was a dream come true," Stephenson said. "I was tending bar in center city and I knew Wheels (Phillies' broadcaster Chris Wheeler). I told him besides bartending I did video work. Wheels said that the Phillies' new owners needed someone to handle the video for them. I ignored him because I didn't think he was serious. Larry Shenk came into the restaurant and asked if I was the video guy that Chris Wheeler mentioned."

Stevenson was hired and went to work for the Phillies. He went to spring training and met Richie Ashburn. "As a kid, I listened to Richie Ashburn. He was the most down-to-earth person. He was very approachable. He considered himself one of the employees. He would be in the employees' dining room and you could go up and talk to him. That is what I enjoyed about Richie, he was a man of the people. That is how he was raised. There was never any pretense. Everyone understood where he fit in around the Phillies. He was the most beloved player in the city.

"Where he grew up was so radically different than this city. He was laid back and easy going. You would think it would have been impossible for him to fit in this city as easily as he did. He was called the city's adopted son. Many people wanted the new ballpark named for Richie but the naming rights were too lucrative.

"Everyone who came into contact with him loved him. He was funny. He would joke about how much he hated pitchers, including his friend Robin Roberts.

"When we were making the DVD on Richie, a 90-second clip of Richie moved David Montgomery to tears. Believe me,

Richie was one of the few people who could have moved David so. He is a businessman who keeps his cool. Ray Didinger (sportswriter and radio personality) talked about Richie's writing career. He talked about when a ghost writer was suggested for Richie, Richie said he wouldn't have his name on the column unless he wrote it. Richie put a lot of hard work into the column. Ray turned into a nine-year-old kid talking about Richie and the way he wore his cap and held his bat. That moment was neat for me.

"I'd remembered someone trying to help Richie get into the Hall of Fame. I had him on the list to be contacted. Jim Donahue offered his views on the grass roots campaign. Jim came in and he had a great story to tell. Jim was 'Joe Everyman.'

"Richie, humorously, would express contempt for the Hall of Fame induction and threaten not to go. Larry Shenk told him that he would deprive himself and his family of the greatest day of their lives. The day was special. Richie received his just reward and he lived to enjoy the day. Sadly, sometimes players are inducted posthumously. His mother was there and they had such a close relationship.

"At the end of the video there is a scene shot at Tilden in the cemetery where his father made many of the gravestones. It's beautiful and peaceful."

* * *

Two weeks after the funeral Jim Donahue received a call from Richie's mother, Toots. "She left a message on my answering machine on a Saturday afternoon and I called her back," Jim said. "She wanted to ask me what I thought of the ceremony for Richie. She wanted to know if it was too much. That is what I loved about her. She was a plain, down-to-earth woman. She asked me if I ever received one of the pins from Cooperstown. They did some special pins for the family members. They have little gold baseballs in the center. When

I said I didn't, she said she would have one sent to me. That was tremendous for me. I still have it in the original box. I also have all of her letters. She died several years after Richie."

* * *

After the funeral and the call from Richie's mother, Jim's connections with the Ashburn family dwindled. "My life shifted gears and calmed down," Jim said. "My daughter and son went to college."

Jim recalls being a part of the Stephenson video on Richie Ashburn. "Dan is a big fan of Richie. I saw a reference that the Phillies were making a video of Richie and Joan wondered why I hadn't been contacted. The next day Dan called and said he had been looking for me for six months. He had tracked me down through author Frank Zimniuch, who included me in his book, *Richie Ashburn Remembered*. The 2007 season was winding down and I went to the stadium and did an interview. The film is sometimes used during rain delays of Phillies' games. I know when it is being played as people will call, telling me they saw me on television."

* * *

Jim did have another goal involving the Phillies; he always wanted to work for the team.

"The first time I talked with Mr. Giles, I said I always loved the Phillies. I just waited for the right circumstances. Working for them was on my bucket list. In 2009 after driving Heather back to the airport after a visit, I decided to drive to the Phillies' office and obtain an employment application. I did so and filled it out.

"I gave Dan Stephenson as a reference. I also attached a press clipping from the Richie campaign. I went for my interview and the two supervisors doing the interview were aware of the Why the Hall Not? campaign. I was told I would hear from them in seven to ten days. I felt I had done well on the interview."

Donahue received a call telling him he would begin work as a game day employee during the 2010 season.

"I enjoy being around the ballpark and helping the fans. The fans are guests and we are told to treat them as guests. We are part of the park experience. You don't have an experience often where you work at a place where 45,000 people arrive happy and most leave happy. The Phillies is a great organization."

"I love my job. I hope to do it for many more years."

* * *

Looking back, Jim Donahue the baseball fan has a cherished memory in which he played a part.

"I'm most proud of seeing Richie enjoying the last two years of his life as a member of the Hall of Fame."

AFTERWORD

THIS BOOK, *Richie Ashburn . . . Why the Hall Not?: The Amazing Journey to Cooperstown*, was destined to be written. Too many instances of happenstance took place to ignore.

The first random event was Jim Donahue's father's obtaining tickets to a game involving the Philadelphia Phillies and the Cincinnati Reds in July 1957. Before the contest, the young fan had a chance to meet one of the star players of the Phillies, Richie Ashburn. Ashburn was a Whiz Kid and one of the stars of not only the Phillies, but also the major leagues. He was a batting champion and an All-Star.

Ashburn was also a country gentleman with a quick wit and smile. He spent a few moments with Jim, had a brief conversation and signed an autograph. The kindness was never forgotten.

Richie Ashburn continued his major league career with the Chicago Cubs and then became a member of the expansion New York Mets, a team remembered for being the most inept group of players in the sport's history. All the losses were too much for the proud and competitive Ashburn. He retired from the Mets after being named the Most Valuable Player on the team that lost the most games ever in one season in the major leagues.

The second event leading to this book came with a decision made by Ashburn during the days leading to spring training of his first year of retirement. He had been thinking about dabbling in politics and running for Congress. Instead, the baseball bug was too much for Ashburn and he accepted an offer by the Phillies to become a member of the team's broadcast crew.

Richie Ashburn was back in Philadelphia and back in baseball.

Ashburn became as revered in Philadelphia for his broadcasting style as he was for his playing style. He was friendly, opinionated and articulate in the booth. Ashburn became a family member to many fans across the Delaware Valley. He was in their living rooms and kitchens every day of the baseball season. From spring until fall, Richie was part of the lives of the fans.

He was also a fan of the game. Ashburn was a professional who understood how the game should be played. When he saw players not putting forth a maximum effort or not playing the game up to his expectations, he told his listeners. The Philadelphia fans admired his honesty and intensity.

When Harry Kalas departed the Houston franchise and joined the Phillies' broadcast team, the club had what many believe was the best broadcasting duo in the history of baseball. Harry and Richie, known for years as Whitey because of the color of his hair, were friends and their broadcasts showcased their special relationship.

Richie Ashburn had the baseball credentials to become a member of the Hall of Fame but not enough baseball writers deemed him worthy of a spot in Cooperstown. A rule change by Major League Baseball seemed to lock the door to the Hall of Fame forever on one of the stars of the 1950's, the same decade that produced legends Mickey Mantle, Willie Mays, Duke Snider and other stars.

Jim Donahue took the next step in this saga by re-establishing contact with Richie Ashburn. Donahue re-introduced himself to Richie during a sports memorabilia show in New Jersey. Ashburn was as gracious as ever when Donahue re-introduced himself.

On the spur of the moment, Donahue decided to launch a campaign to have Major League Baseball change a rule and have Ashburn once again eligible for the Hall of Fame. Donahue asked Ashburn if he objected to his conducting such a campaign. Ashburn thought Donahue was nuts and told him so, but Richie also told Donahue that he couldn't stop him from trying.

The *Why the Hall Not?* grass-roots campaign was launched. Donahue had no contacts with the Hall of Fame, Major League Baseball or the Phillies. The lack of connections didn't deter Donahue. He ran what amounted to a solo campaign that gained prodigious results. Donahue's efforts resulted in almost 200,000 Richie Ashburn supporters signing petitions and postcards urging the Hall of Fame to allow Ashburn to be considered for a spot in Cooperstown.

This book tells Donahue's story of his one-fan campaign that took years to be successful and the star player, Richie "Whitey" Ashburn.

The young life of my co-author Jim Donahue paralleled many aspects of my own. As a youngster Jim looked forward to a trip to Connie Mack Stadium with great anticipation. The chance to meet a major league baseball star, such as Richie Ashburn, would be the highlight of any young fan's life,

Living in rural Chester County, a trip to Connie Mack Stadium at 21st Street and Lehigh Avenue in the big city of Philadelphia was special for me. I anticipated the trips for weeks when my father obtained tickets. I remember drives from my home in Westwood to the Schuylkill Expressway and on to the ball yard. I remember parking in the residential neighborhood where Connie Mack Stadium stood and entering the venerable park. The manicured green grass was always special and it didn't really matter if a pole obstructed the view of part of the field. As a youngster, it also didn't matter if the Phillies was a great team, a mediocre team or a poor one. Being at a major league ball park and watching major league players perform was special.

The food was especially good, at least to the uncultured taste buds of a young fan. The hot dogs were a staple but the hoagies on Amoroso rolls were the best. A Philadelphia soft pretzel purchased from a street vendor was a treat for the ride home.

A special thrill took place after the game. One of the exits went through the right field bullpen and fans could actually walk over the bullpen pitching rubber, the one used by major league pitchers, on their way to their cars. Even if my father's car was parked on the opposite side of the stadium, the right field exit was my favored one. Being able to touch a part of the sacred field allowed a young fan to be part of the game.

Unlike Jim Donahue, I didn't meet Richie Ashburn or any other member of the Philadelphia Phillies. I didn't collect autographs. I played baseball but not nearly well enough to advance past the youth sports leagues. I was the typical "good field, no hit" player.

I stayed connected to the game and sports. My first job was secured by my father with a newspaper where he was employed, the *Coatesville Record*. I began working in the press room as I was filling in for an injured employee who poured hot metal down his boot. My father mentioned to Editor Ralph Flammino that I wrote for the high school newspaper. Flammino, a former football player at Penn State, needed someone to cover high school football. My sports writing career was born.

Besides football, I covered baseball. I remember sitting in the sun at various fields surrounding Coatesville and watching youth, high school and adult league games. I always thought my retirement job would be watching baseball games and writing for a newspaper. Alas, newspapers are quickly fading from the scene.

I met Jim Donahue on Saturday, May 22, 2010. The meeting was another serendipitous event. My wife Katherine Harlan won the chance to purchase tickets from the Chester County Intermediate Unit, where she worked. The tickets were for the game between the Phillies and Boston Red Sox. We arrived early for the game at Citizens Bank Park in South Philadelphia. Our tickets were seats 13 and 14 in row 25 of section 112. The game-day employee handling the usher duties for the Phillies in that section was Jim Donahue. We arrived early and had a chance to meet and talk with Donahue. He was friendly and Katherine made a comment to Donahue about enjoying his work.

Jim told us about his love of the game. At some point, he asked what I did for a living and I said I wrote books. He said he had a book and he did—the *Why the Hall Not?* campaign. The conversation before the Phillies-Red Sox game led to a meeting on June 16 at a restaurant on East State Street in Media, Pennsylvania, appropriately named Quotations. The meeting over sandwiches led to an agreement to tell Jim's story of his relationship with Richie Ashburn.

As I discussed the Ashburn project with a number of people, it was evident Ashburn was still revered in Philadelphia. The feeling was put into words by Tim McCarver, former major league catcher and baseball announcer. On Saturday, July 24, 2010, I was in San Antonio, Texas on some family business and a chance to watch a little of the Phillies game against the Colorado Rockies.

McCarver was one of the announcers for the game. The Phillies were cruising to a 10-2 victory behind the pitching of Kyle Kendrick. As the television camera focused on Ashburn Alley at Citizens Bank Park, McCarver began talking about Ashburn and called Richie one of the most beloved players ever to wear a Philadelphia uniform.

Because of my prior book *Jailing the Johnston Gang: Bringing Serial Murderers to Justice,* published by Barricade Books, Publisher Carole Stuart and I discussed during another true crime book but the project didn't materialize. When I told her of the Ashburn project, she reviewed the *Why the Hall Not?* book proposal and agreed to publish this work.

Stories concerning Richie Ashburn have been reported in numerous newspapers, on websites and other publications. The research for this book included those publications and first-hand accounts from persons who knew Richie Ashburn. Other sources were consulted and when accounts verified, used. A research source list is provided at the conclusion of the book.

This book is the story of All-Star Richie "Whitey" Ashburn and a baseball fan, Jim Donahue.

Bruce Mowday
March 2011

APPENDIX

**Text of Don Richard Ashburn's
Hall of Fame Speech
Made at Cooperstown, New York
On July 30, 1995**
(Source Baseball Hall of Fame Website)

"Thank you, thank you. (applause still) Thank you, thank you. (applause still) Thanks folks. (applause still) Thank you. (applause) Thank you. I'm trying to figure out why everybody that comes up here says, "What took you so long." Ed? No, just kidding. I'm not gonna say that because I'm so happy to be here. Ed called me this spring, Ed, you should call more often, I enjoyed our visit, and gave me the good news and it's really changed my life a lot, it's changed my family's life a lot.

"I can't believe the number of people here today. Happy to see it. (applause builds) Pennsylvania, Delaware, New Jersey. Have a lot of Nebraska people here. One of them I have to introduce to you. Mom? (Applause) 91 year old mother . . . who . . . who, believe me, is a saint. My . . . , I have a brother here, Bob, and Betty my sister, from Nebraska. I have my family here. My wife Herbie, the daughters, Genie, Sue Ann, and Karen, and their families. My two sons, Richard and John, and their wives. A lot of cousins, a lot of nieces and nephews from the great state of Nebraska came here, over a hundred of them, in force. (applause) And you . . . , you Penn Staters should never forget, we're number one. I don't know where. (boos from crowd).

"I . . . ideally, ideally for me this could have happened earlier because, my father's passed away, (Ashburn collects himself), hang on, my twin sister passed away, and we had a daughter, (pause) but . . . on the other hand our grandchildren are here, they wouldn't have been here twenty years ago. We have . . . we have nine of them. I think seven of them are here, all except the two . . . little ones. So that's a nice thing that's happened that they're here to be a part of this.

"Another great thing is I got to go in with Schmitty. (applause) Now . . . you don't plan something like this. You know this is, you can't orchestrate. Mike of course going in on the first ballot, I went in twenty some years later. Nobody could ever plan anything like that, but, but it is a tremendous privilege to go in with Mike. It would have been a tremendous privilege to go in with Steve Carlton who went in last year, and it's nice also that my old teammate, Robin Roberts, who is in, is here today.

"I saw, I saw Schmitty play every game he played. I saw, I saw him from the get go when his manager said `I'd trade Mike Schmidt for a load of pumpkins.' (laughter) I won't tell you who the manager was. (Ashburn laughing) But . . . , Schmitty was always a great fielder right from the get go, no problems with the glove, he had a little trouble early, you know, with the bat, but I saw him improve and work and develop every year until he became the great player that we saw for so many years. And, and Mike it's a real treat to go in here with you today, I'm . . . I'm sincere about it, and I congratulate your mother and Dad and Donna and the kids. (applause) It was a . . . it was a privilege to have seen Schmitty and Steve Carlton, the two greatest I've seen in Phillies uniform. (applause) I can't believe . . . I can't believe this, this great turnout, I, I was just told by Ed here that it's the greatest crowd in the history of the Hall of Fame. (applause is big) Wish I could tell you that we had Tastykakes and pretzels out there, but, but I think you're on your own in that department, but, it's so wonderful to see this many people.

"Wonderful to see the greatest manager I, I ever played for, Eddie Sawyer, who's sitting back here. (applause) Stand up Eddie, would ya? I . . . there's Eddie. I . . . I started my professional career in Utica, New York, which is, you know, just up the road here. Started with Eddie Sawyer in the old Eastern League in 1945. And we had a hell of a ballclub Eddie. But every young player should've had the opportunity to start playing professional ball for a guy like Eddie Sawyer. I played for him in the minors and part of my major league career. A wonderful person who, who taught us so much, and was so good to all of us young people who were involved with the Utica Blue Sox at that time. Eddie, it's really good to see ya here.

"I want to thank the Carpenters, I see Ruly sitting over here, the Carpenter family who did so much for me and my family. The Bill Giles group now, with all the owners here who came up here to see this, who did so much for us here. I want to thank these guys back here, who have made me feel so comfortable. I really didn't feel that comfortable coming up here, it's no secret. They didn't exactly carry me in here on a sedan chair with blazing, er blaring trumpets. (laughter) So I was a little shaky about joining this select group, and they have really been nice to all of us here, and I appreciate it.

"Some of you guys, some of you guys I played against, and I know why you're here, I'm not always sure why I'm here. I would have been here earlier if it wouldn't have been for some of these guys sitting behind me. They always said . . . they always said . . . the thing that's kept you out of here is Mickey, Willie, and the Duke. Well, I don't know about that. There's some other ball players that I think have been overlooked. I'm not a crusader, but I would mention . . . I think Ronnie Santo was overlooked because of . . . Ernie Banks, I think

Vada Pinson was overlooked because of Frank Robinson. Some great ballplayers are there, I think Jim Bunning and Nellie Fox someday will go in there anyway. Aren't in yet, but I think they will. Nellie Fox, one of my dear and good friends, I'd like to see that happen to him one of these days. Somebody oughta check the record of our good friend Rusty Staub, I mean there's some great, great players out there. Well I'm not going to get into that, that's not, that's really not any of my business. I guess I already did. But, that's not up to me but . . . but, there were some beautiful ballplayers who I think should probably be sitting up here . . . someday. (crowd calls for Pete Rose) No, that will be covered, I can guarantee you. (applause, cheers) But . . . but . . . but not by me. I'll let the person who should mention something like that talk about it, but it's not me, and you will hear about it, I'm sure.

"I tell you, the, the greatest part about this day are the fans. I mean really, I mean this is, this is awesome, this is awesome. And you know, I hope that baseball will pay attention a little bit to what has happened here today. I think there's a message here. I mean we hear so many things about what's wrong with baseball. You people aren't here because they're having fireworks tonight. You're not here because they gave something away. Really not here to see a ball game. You're here for the baseball game. And I think that's a message that you send, that maybe we oughta get some things straightened out. You know we're all in this together. I'm talking about the baseball owners, the baseball players, the guys like us who are the veterans. We're in it together, we're in together with the fans. Listen to the fans, (applause), I mean let's don't have . . . let's don't have, let's get this mess straightened out. We're sitting here, we're sitting here without an agreement, we're sitting out here without a baseball commissioner. I can't believe this. (ovation) Thank you, thank you. Thank you.

"I just want to close . . . I just want to close by quoting Casey Stengel, who I played for on the 1962 Mets. It's his birthday today, believe it or not. I think he was born in 1892, but it's Casey Stengel's birthday. The last game of the 1962 New York Mets, the worst team ever put together in the history of baseball. I was the most valuable player on that team, I want you to know. (laughter) We're playing the Chicago Cubs in Chicago, we're down by one run, we get a run, Sammy Drake leads off with a single, I, I followed with a single, my last major league hit because I retired after that season. First and second, and nobody out, Joe Pignatano hit what appeared to be a sure base hit, a little semi-line drive in shallow right-center field. Sammy Drake takes off from second, I take off from first. Kenny Hubbs, who died a year later in a plane crash, great fielder, ran back on the dead run, he caught the ball in the web in his glove, he turned over about six times and held on to the ball, threw it to second, second out, back to first, triple play, ended our season, our 120th loss. (laughter) A major league record. As we walked into the visitors clubhouse Casey Stengel was standing there. And he said to us, he said, 'Fellers,' he says, 'I don't want anybody to feel bad about this,' he said, 'this has been a real team effort.' (laughter) He said, 'No one or two people could have done all this.' Well, that, that's what I . . . I'm going to quote Casey, no one or two people could have done all this, and everybody that had a part of it, God bless, and especially the fans, you have made this the greatest day of my life."

CAREER STATS

- Full Name: **Don "Whitey" Richard Ashburn**
- Born: **March 19, 1927 in Tilden, NE**
- Height: **5' 10"**
- Weight: **170**
- Bats: **Left**
- Throws: **Right**
- College: **N/A**
- MLB Debut: **April 20, 1948**

SEASON	TEAM	G	AB	R	H	TB	2B	3B	HR	RBI	BB	IBB	SO	SB	CS	AVG	OBP	SLG	OPS	GO/AO
1948	PHI	117	463	78	154	185	17	4	2	40	60		22	32		.333	.410	.400	.810	
1949	PHI	154	662	84	188	231	18	11	1	37	58		38	9		.284	.343	.349	.692	
1950	PHI	151	594	84	180	239	25	14	2	41	63		32	14		.303	.372	.402	.774	
1951	PHI	154	643	92	221	274	31	5	4	63	50		37	29	6	.344	.393	.426	.819	
1952	PHI	154	613	93	173	219	31	6	1	42	75		30	16	11	.282	.362	.357	.720	
1953	PHI	156	622	110	205	254	25	9	2	57	61		35	14	6	.330	.394	.408	.802	
1954	PHI	153	559	111	175	210	16	8	1	41	125		46	11	8	.313	.441	.376	.817	
1955	PHI	140	533	91	180	239	32	9	3	42	105	5	36	12	10	.338	.449	.448	.897	
1956	PHI	154	628	94	190	241	26	8	3	50	79	3	45	10	1	.303	.384	.384	.768	
1957	PHI	156	626	93	186	228	26	8	0	33	94	1	44	13	10	.297	.390	.364	.754	
1958	PHI	152	615	98	215	271	24	13	2	33	97	7	48	30	12	.350	.440	.441	.881	
1959	PHI	153	564	86	150	173	16	2	1	20	79	4	42	9	11	.266	.360	.307	.667	
1960	CHC	151	547	99	159	185	16	5	0	40	116	1	50	16	4	.291	.415	.338	.753	
1961	CHC	109	307	49	79	94	7	4	0	19	55	2	27	7	6	.257	.373	.306	.679	
1962	NYM	135	389	60	119	153	7	3	7	28	81	2	39	12	7	.306	.424	.393	.817	
CAREER		2189	8365	1322	2574	3196	317	109	29	586	1198	25	571	234	92	.308	.396	.382	.778	

Richie Ashburn Timeline

1927	Born March 19, 1927, in Tilden, Nebraska
1945	Signed by the Philadelphia Phillies
1948	Made Major League debut on April 20, 1948
	Named to National League All-Star team as a rookie
1949	Married Herbie Cox on November 6, 1949
1950	Became member of Phillies National League champions The Whiz Kids
1951	Named to National League All-Star team
1953	Named to National League All-Star team
1955	Became National League Batting Champion with .338 average
1958	Named to National League All-Star team
	Became National League Batting Champion with .380 average
1960	Traded to Chicago Cubs on January 11, 1960
1961	Purchased by New York Mets on December 8, 1961
1962	Named to National League All-Star team
	Made final Major League game appearance on September 30, 1962
	Named Most Valuable Player on New York Mets
1963	Became a broadcaster for Philadelphia Phillies
1995	Inducted into the Hall of Fame on July 30, 1995
1997	Died September 9, 1997, in New York City
	Buried in Gladwyne Methodist Church Cemetery, Gladwyne, Pennsylvania
2004	Honored by Ashburn Alley in Citizens Bank Park which opened April 12, 2004

Whitey & Harry
By Chuck Brodsky

Moonlight on the mountains
North Carolina two-lane
Trying to find a ballgame
No matter how bad the reception
Whitey, man, I miss you
When I listen to the Phillies
And there's Harry going on without you
Harry . . . good old Harry

Radio under my pillow
Kept me up on school nights
The ballgames from the west coast
Wouldn't start until eleven
Whitey, man, I miss you
When I listen to the Phillies
And there's Harry going on without you
For the first time since I was seven

We wore red, the thousands of us
Who'd come to say goodbye & pay their last respects
This tough town really loved you
I saw grown men who wept

Bats & spikes & flowers
Made a shrine around your casket
And I signed in in the guestbook
As the line filed past it
Whitey, man, I miss you
When I listen to the Phillies
And there's Harry going on without you
Harry . . . good old Harry

He Wore Number One
By Skip Denenberg and Tom Burgoyne

So many of us still remember, but then, how could we ever forget,
that fair haired boy from a small town out in the mid west
who came and saw and conquered, and made this town his home
and brought us all together and we embraced him as our own

and from the farming fields of Nebraska, to the glow of those big
    city lights
he could make us believe in the magic and shine as bright
and we'd cheer as he rounded the bases
and when he stepped up to the plate
right along with the smiles on our faces we called him great

and he wore number one, like it was meant to be
yeah he wore number one, when he won the heart of the city

it's written down in Cooperstown for all the world to see
and pressed between the pages of our memories
we all grew up together, that's how it seemed to me
a stronger bond than friendship, more like family

and we share more than moments together
in a way that still matters so much
to this day we all say he's remembered as one of us
he was there in our shiny new Buicks and in our beat up old
    Chevrolet's
on our front steps and our kitchen tables to end our days

and he wore number one like it was meant to be
yeah he wore number one when he won the heart of the city

through the years the way we feel remains the same
and the kid's from here to Tilden need to know his name

cause he was number one and he will always be
yeah he was number one when he won the heart of the city
yeah he was number one, when he won the heart of the city

ACKNOWLEDGMENTS

BOOKS ARE ALWAYS a team project. Just as Richie Ashburn was an All-Star member of the Phillies, many people contributed to the writing of *Richie Ashburn . . . Why the Hall Not?: The Amazing Journey to Cooperstown.*

The book is built around the recollections of Jim Donahue, the baseball fan who was befriended by a star Phillies player Richie Ashburn. Donahue then spearheaded a grassroots campaign to rally support for Richie's deserved spot in the Hall of Fame. Donahue spent a number of hours retelling his story for this book.

Jim Donahue thanks his wife Joan for her love, and her belief in his "hare-brained" ideas. He also acknowledges his children, Heather, Ryan and Caitlin and urges them never to stop pursuing their dreams. To every fan who signed the Richie Ashburn petition or put a bumper sticker on his car, Jim thanks them and tells them they truly made a difference.

My wife Katherine Harlan began the conversation with Jim Donahue about his work as a Phillies game day employee during a game involving the Phillies and Boston Red Sox. That conversation led to my participation in this book. Katherine is also an excellent proofreader and worked her magic on this manuscript.

Barricade Books Publisher Carole Stuart embraced the Ashburn book project and offered excellent publishing assistance, just as she did with my previous book for Barricade, *Jailing the Johnston Gang: Bringing Serial Murderers to Justice.*

A number of friends with major league contacts helped me on the research of this book. They are Norm Mawby, Carl Francis, Matt Coyne, Mike Boettcher, Tim Connor and

Mike Herron. Norm wrote his own successful book on the employees of the Phillies and used his contacts to introduce me to Phillies team officials. He also shared with me his Richie Ashburn Hall of Fame induction day commemorative pin.

Carl and Matt introduced me to their front-office Phillies' contacts. Mike Boettcher asked Chris Wheeler to help with book. Mike Herron is a long-time friend of Ted Spencer, former curator of the National Baseball Hall of Fame and Museum in Cooperstown, New York. Mike Herron and I spent two days in Cooperstown reviewing information on Ashburn. Ted Spencer opened doors at the Hall of Fame Library and sat for an interview for this book. Tim Wiles, Director of Research, and his staff were very helpful in pulling information on Richie Ashburn from the files of the Hall of Fame.

When Tim Conner found out I was researching a book on Richie Ashburn, he reached out to Richie's daughter, Jean Ashburn. I also want to thank Jean Ashburn for taking the time to talk to me about her father and the Why the Hall Not? campaign. I wish her luck on her book project concerning her father.

Dan Stephenson of the Philadelphia Phillies wrote the introduction to this book and he also was interviewed for the text. Dan is a Phillies fan along with being an employee of the Philadelphia Phillies. Dan was the producer of a fine DVD *Richie Ashburn: A Baseball Life.* The video is available through the Phillies website and at Citizens Bank Park. Dan's help and comments are appreciated.

Larry Shenk, a valued member of the Phillies front-office team for many years, took time off from his busy life to be interviewed. His taking time to be asked questions is appreciated. Chris Wheeler also spent part of a Sunday afternoon being interviewed about his friend, Richie Ashburn. He also kindly offered the use of stories from his fine book, *View From the Booth.*

Chuck Brodsky of Ashville, North Carolina, wrote a song called *Whitey and Harry* and gave permission for the printing of the lyrics in this book. Chuck's work can be found at *www.chuckbrodsky.com*. Skip Denenberg and Tom Burgoyne also gave permission for their song, *He Wore Number One*, to be used in this book.

Ted Taylor was instrumental in promoting the Why the Hall Not? campaign and he also sat for an interview for this book. Ted is an expert on sports memorabilia and collecting and has written newspaper columns and hosted radio shows.

Many other people contributed their thoughts and encouragement for this book and also demonstrated that there is a market for a book on Richie Ashburn. Wendy Walker, a writer and editor, helped with the organization of an early chapter. Pam Costanzi was one of the first persons that I told about this book. She said the book would be a perfect gift for her father. Many friends and acquaintances have offered the same sentiments.

BIBLIOGRAPHY

THE FOLLOWING ARE the sources used for research for this book.

National Baseball Hall of Fame and Museum, Cooperstown, New York.

Phillies 2010 Media Guide.

Richie Ashburn: A Baseball Life, a DVD produced by Dan Stephenson for the Philadelphia Phillies and Arts Alliance America, 2008.

Richie Ashburn: Remembered by Fran Zimniuch, Sports Publishing L.L.C., Champaign, Ill, 2005.

View From the Booth by Chris Wheeler as told to Hal Gullan. Camino Books, Philadelphia, PA. 2009.

www.basball-Almanac.com, a website of Major League Baseball information.

www.mlb.com, website of Major League Baseball.

www.baseballreference.com, a website containing baseball statistics.

INDEX

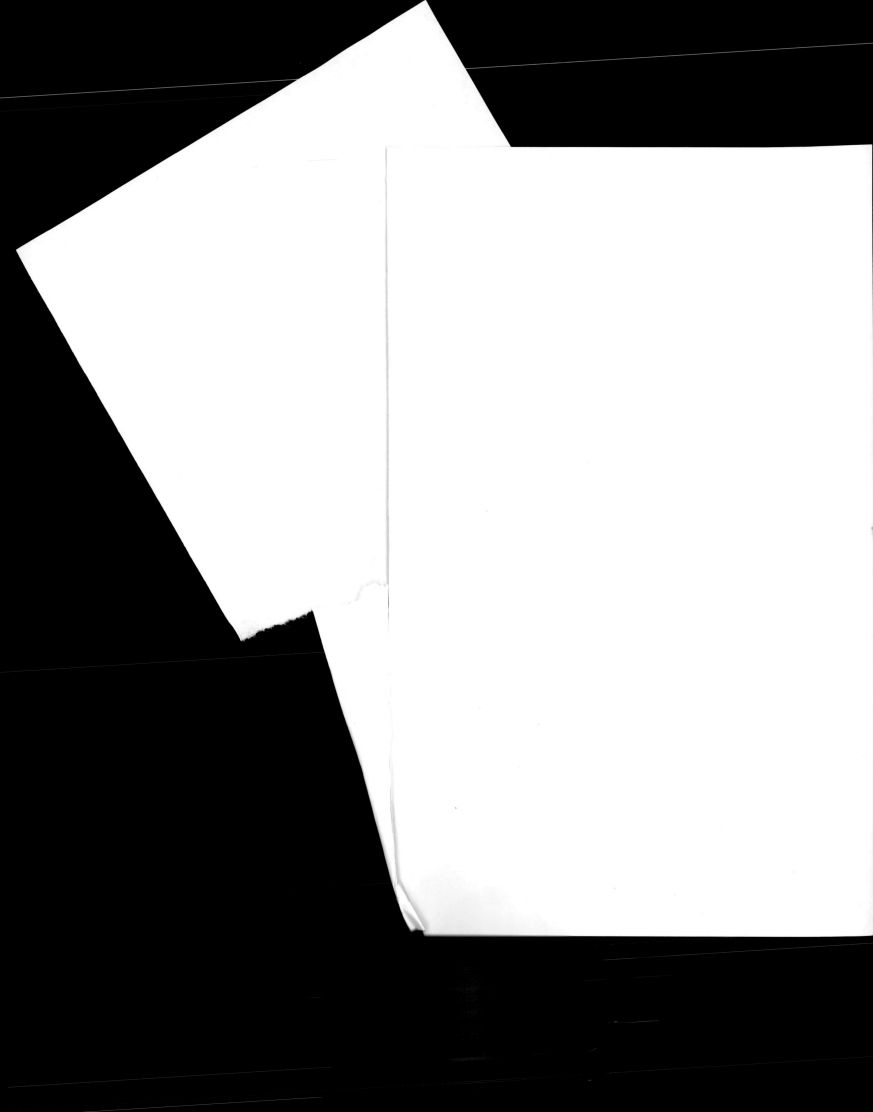